A MILLENNIAL'S GUIDE TO

RUNNING FOR OFFICE

HOW TO GET ELECTED WITHOUT KISSING THE RING

HENRY BOUCHOT

ISBN: 978-1-7350507-1-3

First printing 2021

Cover Design: Vanessa Mendozzi
Typesetting/Interior Design: Stewart A. Williams

Published by John Henry Publishers

JOHN HENRY
PUBLISHERS

CONTENTS

PREFACE

I wrote this book during a two-month sprint starting in October of 2018, a few short months after beating an incumbent, and three other challengers, to become the youngest councilmember in Whittier, California's history. I usually start a new endeavor by reading up on the subject matter. Before the campaign, however, I was unable to find a book that adequately covered the process of running for local elected office from the perspective of a dark horse candidate like me. I was relegated to reinventing the wheel.

In a way, that was just fine for me. From the beginning, I saw my campaign as an opportunity to build something special, to make a difference. I relished the chance to put together an exemplary political campaign, something I could be proud of, win or lose. I looked at the race as an opportunity to test newly acquired skills and achieve something meaningful, the political equivalent of a perfect game in baseball. Just as a pitcher can throw balls during a no-hitter, I also made some mistakes, including worrying too much what gatekeepers think. However, looking back on my experience, I feel that, on the whole, my campaign can serve as a model for what a modern-day race for local office can be.

Politicians certainly love to show off, but this isn't about that for me. This book isn't a tell-all or a memoir, although my personal story will feature predominantly throughout as a jumping-off point. This book is primarily a manual, a guidebook, with an emphasis on the *guide* part. I wrote this book not to impress you, but so that you can learn how to win.

Why do I care if you win or lose? Well, at the risk of sounding melodramatic, because I believe our future depends on you. When I say this, I assume that we're similar in a few crucial ways. First, you may or may not be "young" (this is a millennial's guide, emphasis on the apostrophe, after all, not a millennials' guide), but you're undoubtedly young at heart. By this, I mean, you're tired of elected officials who drive this country as if the gear was stuck in reverse. The promise of the future guides you as much as good times past. You're also a change maker, perhaps even a rule-breaker. You're dissatisfied with the status quo and have a vision for a better future. And you're sick of sitting on the sidelines waiting for that future to come about.

I had a good idea of what I wanted to change when I decided to run. I felt that cities and towns could reduce inequality among its residents while also increasing their happiness.[1] As a Southern California native, I was, and am, optimistic about the incredible potential our region can unlock with reduced traffic and pollution, and an adequate housing supply. Finally, I wanted to demonstrate how people who the president at the time wrote off as rapists and murderers could run an exemplary city.

Back to you. You're a Democrat. Or a Republican. Perhaps even an Independent. Frankly, your party matters less to me than your character. Part of the reason I ran for local office, as opposed to Congress, was how tired I was with how partisan Washington's political climate had become. I have friends from both sides of the aisle. There will always be members of opposing political parties in America. The question is, what kind of leaders are we going to have? That's the goal of this book – to ensure the best type of leaders, the competent and the selfless, are elected. Leaders, of course, are most needed where there are intractable problems to solve. As Martin Luther King, Jr. said, "The ultimate measure of a man is not where he stands in moments of comfort and convenience, but where he stands at times of challenge and controversy. The true neighbor will risk his position, his prestige, and even his life for the welfare of others." You *should* run when you're ready to be a public servant. You *must* run when you're the right person to solve the unsolvable.

For me, the unsolvable was homelessness. In November of 2018, only a few months into my first term, a large encampment formed at the city's largest park, Parnell Park. The Ninth Circuit Court of Appeals in *Martin v. Boise* had decided the month prior that it was a violation of the Constitution's prohibition against cruel and unusual punishment to enforce overnight camping and vagrancy laws without sufficient bed space for each homeless resident. (During the summer of 2018, I had been the sole vote against the city's homelessness plan[2] because I felt it lacked a concrete plan to create such space). In December, a second encampment formed in the middle of a large median on Whittier Boulevard, for every commuter to see.[3]

My steadfast support for a homeless shelter placed me at odds with a considerable portion of the community and made me anathema to many voters. People posted screenshots of my house on social media saying I should have the homeless move in with my family and me, they wagged fingers at me at council meetings, and they depicted me as a traitor and a buffoon. Our civic norms were clearly eroding, with homelessness acting as the flashpoint. It seemed to me that their anger belied a fear of losing control. As I described in a letter for a collection dubbed "Dear Whittier," Whittierites don't easily embrace change:

> A second key characteristic of Whittierites is their profound longing for the past. This longing explains the proliferation of online sites dedicated to satisfying their nostalgia pangs. Just as Whittierites are prone to embrace the idea that locally grown solutions are superior, so are they instinctively inclined to look to the past for answers: "If you just left things how they were" is the Whittierite's exasperated refrain.
>
> These two characteristics – exceptionalism and nostalgia – are frequently in conflict. Whittierites demand only the best but often balk at the tradeoffs. When they do begrudgingly make a change, the new status quo eventually becomes deeply entrenched.

Doing nothing doesn't make a problem go away, though. It only gets worse. So, I took it upon myself to break the logjam. I began to work on a compromise plan. Working with Federal District Judge David O. Carter, a Vietnam Marine, I was able to bring the city a solution. The agreement would allow us to enforce our anti-camping laws once again in exchange for providing shelter beds for 60% of our homeless population.

Fast forward to September 2020: our council voted unanimously to approve a 139-bed homeless shelter,[4] which the community mainly supports, and the media is praising Whittier for being a leader on homelessness.[5] Our shelter opened just a few days before the hottest day in the history of Los Angeles, with temperatures reaching 111-degrees and with fires to the north covering cars with ashes. To the chagrin of those who maintained that homeless people don't want help, 122 of the 158 unsheltered residents in Whittier accepted our offer of housing.

Now, I was in the Marines. I've served with some real heroes. And I don't consider myself one. Yet I'm reasonably sure that this particular, deeply entrenched problem wouldn't have been addressed without my help. As Thomas Jefferson stated, "One man with courage is a majority." Ultimately, I wrote this book hoping it finds its way into the hands of a few majorities of one.

INTRODUCTION

It's a well-worn truth that all politics is local. You could imagine a political system where, as in a professional sports draft, the worst-off cities have the best chance of picking top talent. Instead, our representatives are supposed to be homegrown. Although carpetbaggers occasionally win, voters typically reject Johnny-come-latelies. Good candidates, by necessity, must know the ins and outs of their jurisdictions. Great candidates love where they live, sincerely want to make it better, and convince others of their ability to create that change.

My love affair with Whittier started on Saturday, June 29, 2013. My oldest friend Jay got married that day. A power forward with a sweet jump shot, he's been the Shaq to my Kobe since we ran the blacktops of East L.A. Light & Life Christian School. The wedding reception was at the Harmony Center for Spiritual Living, a stucco building in Whittier on the corner of Bailey and Comstock, which is adorned with a painting of a large blue and red heart that resembles a Jackson Pollock painting.

I knew about Whittier from having gone to high school at Schurr in nearby Montebello. I considered Whittier "boujee." I had grown up in Boyle Heights, a Los Angeles neighborhood just east of Downtown, where about 95% of the population is Latino. In the gang flick *Blood in Blood Out*, Miklo responds to a question from his ride home about how that neighborhood differs from L.A. proper with, "It's a whole different country." I felt similarly about Whittier. To me, it was la-la land, a place where you needn't worry about gang affiliation or robbery. With its turn-of-the-century bungalows, leafy parks, and old churches, it seemed like Mayberry to me.

With a few hours to kill between Jay and Denise's wedding ceremony and the reception, my wife, Christina, and I decided to explore. We bought a couple of lawn chairs at a drug store and found some nearby green space at Founders Park, a converted cemetery. We read the relocated deceased's names on the large, marble headstone and gazed at the Spanish Revival, Craftsman, and Tudor homes.

With a baby on the way, I knew a single-family residence was in the cards. I'd been reading a book called *The Just Right Home* by Marianne Cusato and was enamored with the idea of finding a home in a walkable, inner ring, turn-of-the-century suburb. Except I was getting ready to deploy to Afghanistan as a Marine Judge Advocate in September 2013 and the idea of going through escrow seemed inconceivable. My curiosity got the best of me, though. I whipped out my smartphone and checked for nearby open houses.

The closest home for sale was a barn-red, 1909 bungalow with a wide front porch and overhanging eaves. It was like stepping into the past as Christina and I walked through the oversized screen door with its original hardwood floors, wooden rafters, built-in bookshelves, and bench seats. Without air conditioning, it was also unbelievably hot. We fell in love with the house, but it was over budget, and I was about to spend a month in the Mojave Desert on a pre-deployment exercise. Two weeks and a couple of price-drops later, and we had an offer in, me withstanding 124-degree heat to find a single bar of cellphone reception so I could communicate with our realtor and lender during negotiations.

It seemed a little silly at the time to pay for a home that would lay empty for months as I left for Helmand Province and Christina went home to Connecticut to give birth. However, I knew that we had made the right decision the day I came home from Afghanistan. I woke up in the middle of the night and walked to the Winchell's Donuts, which stays open 24 hours, about three blocks from our new home. I remember being stunned by the quiet, by the song of the birds. It was peace. No controlled detonations, no rocket attacks, and no radio at my side, just birds and trees. I could finally exhale.

In a way, the relationship I have with the town of Whittier is like any close relationship. You're infatuated at first, and then, as intimacy increases, you discover what's underneath the façade. In the ensuing years, I would find out just how much I had to learn about Whittier, the place I had decided to make my permanent residence and where I would eventually run for city council.

Whittier is about a dozen miles southeast of Downtown Los Angeles as the crow flies. According to the Census Bureau, 86,064 people resided in Whittier as of 2018. It's a fairly large town geographically at just under fifteen square miles. The San Gabriel River to the west and the Puente Hills Habitat, a nature preserve, to the north, border Whittier. Unlike Boyle Heights, which is crisscrossed by five freeways, no highway bisects Whittier. This isolation probably explains why Whittier has remained such a backwater – culturally, architecturally, and politically – for so long.

Whittier becomes more affluent as you drive north or east. The farther you move from the south and west parts of town, the less you feel like you're inside older, denser, and more diverse Los Angeles County, and the closer you are to the more affluent, litter-free, whiter, conservative, and more corporate Orange County. Unincorporated areas surround Whittier, a chartered city, on all sides. These areas experience more crime and poverty than Whittier proper.

Whittier has a long, rich history. Midwesterners from a religious sect known as the Quakers, which promote tolerance and religious freedom, founded Whittier. Before them, there were settlements of native Tongva. Early on, Whittier was known for its citrus fruit and nuts until the discovery of oil led to the influx of oilmen, including future president George H.W. Bush.

Speaking of presidents, Richard Nixon grew up in Whittier, received his bachelor's degree at Whittier College, and started his law practice and political career in Whittier. One of Whittier's biggest disappointments was getting passed over for the Nixon Presidential Library in favor of Yorba Linda, his birthplace.[6]

Whittier has plenty of other buildings to be proud of, though. The preservation of its architectural history is one of the main reasons why the word *charm* is so often associated with the city. Its historical buildings include Pio Pico State Park, the ranch owned by California's first governor. There are well-preserved examples of Mid-Century Modern buildings, like City Hall and the Central Library, and plenty of homes in every 20th Century Revival style, particularly on the west end of town. The Bailey House, the

19th-century ranch home belonging to Whittier founder Jonathan Bailey serves as a year-round museum, and the old train depot operates as meeting and office spaces. A developer is converting an eighty-plus acre former youth correctional facility, Fred C. Nelles, one of the first local economic drivers, into 750 new homes and about 200,000 square feet of commercial space while keeping several original structures intact.

Although it's admittedly tricky to get in and out of Whittier, particularly for those on its east end, due to the lack of nearby freeways, there is exciting news on the horizon in terms of public transportation. Whittier was selected to receive a light rail line for the first time in over a half-century with its selection as the terminus of Metro's Gold Line extension. We expect the new rail line to be completed as soon as 2028, in time for the summer Olympics. It will bring increased access to Presbyterian Intercommunity Hospital (PIH), a major job center. There's also the Greenway Trail, a former railroad right of way turned 4.5-mile commuter and recreational bikeway, pedestrian path, and greenbelt. We are extending this path an additional 2.8 miles east to Orange County.

Understanding the built environment and transportation alone isn't enough, of course, to lead a city. You must know its people just as well. The modern story of Whittier's population is the "browning" of its community. Latinos constituted only 23% of Whittier residents in 1980; they were 56% as of 2000. By 2010, Hispanics accounted for almost 66% of the population. In Whittier's high schools today, over 90% of the student body is Latino.

The reduction of the white population in an inner-ring suburb isn't a phenomenon unique to Whittier by any stretch. However, this isn't quite the so-called "white flight" characteristic of postwar America. Whittier isn't a place whites flee from so much as it is a place Latinos head toward, a symbol of Latino upward social mobility. For children of Latin American immigrants, making the eastward trek down Whittier Boulevard, from Boyle Heights and East L.A. through Montebello and Pico Rivera, Whittier is the end of the road; it is Eden, the Latino Beverly Hills.[7] (I like to say I went from *Los Cinco Puntos,* a prominent five-way intersection in Boyle Heights, to Five Points, a prominent five-way intersection in Whittier).

In Whittier, residency is either hard-earned or a birthright. Perhaps because of these circumstances, Whittierites feel strongly that they are special. Even though Whittier, as a middle-class, bedroom community, isn't unlike a thousand other American cities, Whittierites see themselves as a breed apart. It's hard to explain. Here's my best shot in a letter to the Whittier Library for the collection, "Dear Whittier."

A gentleman steps up to the podium during public comment and starts, "I've lived in Whittier for fifty-three years." He is evidently fifty-three years old. He doesn't say much else about himself, his primary qualification being his lifelong residency. Several onlookers nod knowingly, satisfied with his bona fides. He is a true Whittierite, they say to themselves, born and bred, and thus well-versed in the "Whittier Way."

Whittierites possess a deeply ingrained sense of their exceptionalism. They presume that Whittier does it better as you would assume a Laker looks good in gold. Outsiders sometimes mistake this outlook as arrogance. Whittierites aren't boasting, though. They just hold the truth of their excellence to be self-evident. That the girls are simply prettier in Whittier, as they say, is axiomatic.

When I bought a home in Whittier in 2013, I had no idea that the city would take such a central role in my life. Growing up in Boyle Heights, I barely knew my next-door neighbors. Here, I've knocked on thousands of their doors. The idea that I might serve on Whittier's city council wasn't at all on my radar when we moved here. When I did decide to run, though, I knew that winning over Whittierites wasn't going to be a walk in the park. After all, Whittierites have high standards. Having a strong resume and good intentions wasn't going to be enough, just as knowing the history of the people and place wasn't going to be. I'd need to transform myself into the kind of leader the city would need moving forward. The ensuing pages explain how I became that person for my city and how you might also become one for yours.

In Part I, I describe how I decided on running for office, providing you with a framework for making your own choice. In Part II, I explain what mistakes I made coming out of the gate and entering the political world in hopes that you will avoid them. I strongly recommend that you read the first two parts no matter what stage of the process you're in. However, you might want to start with Part III for a "soup to nuts" explanation of everything you need to know to run a successful campaign if your campaign is already underway. I advise you on what to do after the campaign, win or lose, in Part IV.

You can find more information, including checklists, timelines, an online companion course to this book, and other resources at www.authorauthorhenrybouchot.com.

PART I:

DECIDING TO RUN

"One of the penalties for refusing to participate in politics is that
you end up being governed by your inferiors."

– PLATO

CHAPTER 1

DON'T RUN

I think I'm gonna pass out.

These are the words I whisper to my wife, Christina, outside El Camino Mexican Grill, the night of my election. This restaurant is nestled between a salon and a florist in a tiny strip mall on the curved Workman Mill Road, which leads to Rose Hills. With its 700 acres, Rose Hills is the largest cemetery in the United States. The restaurant's owner has John 14:6 emblazoned on the menu. In this verse, Jesus says, "I am the way and the truth and the life. No one comes to the Father except through me." Not another gatekeeper, I think to myself. Facing a nine-term incumbent, I feel like I'm going to need a miracle tonight; Christina tries to calm me down. "Henry, you've done everything you could. You knocked on, what, five thousand doors? You've put everything you had into this. I'm proud of you, honey." She pumps some water into me and makes me take a few deep breaths so I can get inside for the results. That's fine, I think, but what if I lose? Will anyone remember this race? The headstones at Rose Hills bearing names long forgotten cross my mind.

★

It was about a year before my election. I was meeting a young political consultant who was introduced to me by a mutual friend.

We met at the 6740, a sports bar slash dive where they sell *menudo*, a traditional Mexican beef tripe stew made, oddly enough, with tofu. I passed on the *tofudo* and went with a Sam Adams Octoberfest. Danny Fierro, the consultant, had a Guinness. I was excited to meet Danny as I'd been considering running since shortly after my honorable discharge from the Marines. Danny started telling me about the likelihood of beating the thirty-six-year incumbent (low) and the challenges involved (significant). An Ivy League grad, he was the veteran of many a political battle. Despite being only twenty-eight, he had already founded a political consulting firm and had the California Assembly Majority Leader as a client.

I expected Danny to be a hard-nosed type, but I found him self-effacing and sharp, and we hit it off. Although our chances were poor, my resume was good, and there seemed to be a sliver of daylight that I might be able to run through and win in a challenging local race. And then, as he sipped his second pint of beer, he said something that struck me. "Henry, friends don't let friends run for office. The pay sucks, your wife will hate you, and you're going to have difficulty finding a job afterward. Not to mention all the scrutiny you're gonna face." I wish I could say I took Danny's words to heart. I had already made up my mind. I was going to run, and I laughed his words off, figuring they applied to people with thinner skin than me.

Skip ahead to the present day, however, and much of what he said was true. Well, except my wife hating me (I think). Being a local politician is yeoman's work. It's mostly unglamorous and poorly paid. And it's practically impossible to simultaneously hold down a regular full-time job with a commute and raise a family.

On top of that, the process of becoming a public figure is

daunting. The filter typically preventing people from saying mean things to you gets removed when you run. Partly because politicians have come into such a high level of disrepute and partly because a real-life politician is still somewhat of a curiosity, constituents, and even friends, will sometimes give you unvarnished criticism that can smart. Even when people are friendly, it's hard to knock on a door and ask, let alone convince, a stranger to put their neighborhood's fate in your hands.

Once you become a candidate, criticism of you, your family, your business, your past, your relationships, your demeanor, your attitude, experience, dress, way of speaking, your choice of words, platform, and ideas – everything – becomes fair game. People who you trusted will disappoint and, occasionally, backstab you. For some, particularly for the idealists at heart, this can be soul-crushing. And the "fun" doesn't stop if you win. If anything, it intensifies. Better to know what you're getting into, warts and all.

I hate to say it, but I agree with Danny. Don't run for office, especially if your first instinct is to look for what's in it for you. As the sign once greeting Marines at the now-demolished O'Bannon Hall at The Basic School, the Marine officer finishing course, in Quantico, Virginia, states: IT'S NOT ABOUT YOU. I won't go into the cautionary tales of excess, abuse of power, and bribery of which the newspapers are chock-full. Suffice to say that the return on investment is seldom going to work out in your favor unless your concept of "return" is the public good. As my college friend Zuhey Espinoza once told me, you need just "the right mix of altruism and narcissism." I call it *selflishness*.

The starting point for this book is thus not the mechanics of running for office, but rather the personal dimension, *the experience* of running, which in turn depends on your motivations. Running for elected office is truly a life-altering experience comparable (in terms of its impact on you) to that of having a child, losing a parent, or even going to war (believe me, I've experienced all three). It's challenging to succeed in running for local office unless you comprehend the extent to which you'll be challenged, and changed, in the process.

If becoming a politician is a life-altering experience, it's because the people involved make it one. These pages are filled with colorful characters. You might find yourself asking why I cover them in such great detail. While each jurisdiction will invariably have its own cast, certain archetypes commonly appear, including: the young upstart, the longstanding incumbent, the gadfly, the sharp-elbowed climber, the activist, and so on. I would prefer that you learn about, and from, such people in these pages before you must face them in real life.

Not everyone is ready to be an elected official. You must be brutally honest with yourself about this. Have you been through significant adversity in the past, and were you able to overcome it? Because, if not, a campaign for elected office might not the best place to cut your teeth. As for me, I had grown up in one of the toughest neighborhoods in Southern California, Boyle Heights. It felt like I couldn't walk across the street without being stopped and asked whether I was gang-affiliated. My parents were blue-collar, small business types. Had it not been for my father, I might've fallen victim to the street life. I remember how angry I would get with him for forcibly removing the gangbanger-looking baggie jeans I would hide in my backpack. Now, having skirted the gangs of East Los Angeles, I feel blessed for his intervention. I went on to be the first in my family to graduate from college. I then went to law school and joined the Marines as an officer. I ultimately went from being afflicted with imposter syndrome, a frame of mind in which a person doubts their accomplishments and talents and fears being exposed as a fraud, to feeling like I could handle anything life could throw at me. What about you? What adversity have you faced? What experiences will you reach for when times get tough and the path forward becomes murky?

You must also ask yourself whether this is just a whim. With most elected positions requiring a four-year term, entering into politics is a long-term commitment, which is best suited for people with a demonstrated commitment to public service. As a student at Loyola Marymount, a Jesuit university, I had also come to see community service not just as what you did when you racked up too many traffic tickets but as something necessary to developing into a complete person. I spent my free time tutoring elementary school children in Boyle Heights and my spring break rehabbing houses in post-Katrina New Orleans. From college on, service was a way of life for me. Are you committed to public service, or do you just want to be in charge? Believe it or not, it can be hard to tell the difference.

All this to say, be realistic when you consider running for office. Don't just dive in headfirst without thinking. Before you take the plunge, make sure you can confidently answer yes to the following questions: (1) Am I running for the right reasons? (2) Am I the best person for the job? (3) Does my plan give me a reasonable chance of winning? (4) Do I possess a strategic advantage?

SUMMARY

- Being a politician is hard work, and it takes a toll on your personal life.
- When you're a public figure, you become subject to stinging criticism.
- Running is a life-altering decision. Don't decide on a whim, or for selfish reasons.
- A campaign is not the best place to cut your teeth. Make sure you play to win.

RESOURCES

For a decision-making tool on deciding whether to run and other resources, go to authorauthorhenrybouchot.com.

CHAPTER 2

RUN FOR A REASON

If you're sincerely interested in running for office, ask yourself: Am I running because I'm convinced there are specific local policies that are badly in need of change for my community to flourish? Don't run just because you think it might be "fun." And please don't run if you've convinced yourself it would fill some unmet need for validation. Voters in local elections are typically highly invested in their communities and are wary of those who have the wrong idea about local office. They don't want you to "think globally, act locally." "Think locally, act locally" is their creed. They might be Democrats or Republicans, but as taxpayers, they care most about whether you'll protect their interests, primarily those related to their financial wherewithal and quality of life.

Are You a Pragmatist?

More and more, local races have become proxy wars for activists frustrated with federal politics. The relatively low barrier to entry combined with the hyperpartisan lure of beating an actual opponent from across the aisle means ballots are increasingly riddled with candidates long on ardent desire to change society and short on realistic goals. The other issue with local activists, and idealists in general, is that they're prone to developing a martyr complex, preferring a nice, warm blade rather than the hard, sober, pragmatic work of running a winning election.

That's too bad. Local municipal governments carry the lion's share of the responsibilities of providing people with their most cherished services (such as water, heat, police, fire protection, courts, waste removal, parks, and public transportation). They don't need local races to become overly politicized.

I don't mean to say that the same person who is deeply unsatisfied with Washington's current state of affairs has no business running for local elected office. I mean that to be successful, both as a candidate and as an elected official, you must view your race in a hyper-local way. That can mean focusing any number of issues – the overflowing local landfill, unaffordable housing, pockmarked roads, and so on. Just make sure your issues are specific. Generalized dissatisfaction with the status quo and vague social justice recriminations are insufficient. Local anger at the federal government isn't enough either.

What Motivates You?

A person's reasons for running for office can be as varied as people themselves. When I first considered running for office, it was in the context of a California Voting Rights Act lawsuit that had forced our city to end the practice of at-large elections. Whittier broke up into four districts with a citywide mayor. I had bought a house in District 2 in 2013, which would not be contested until 2018 (elections for the first and third districts would be held April 2016). In time, I became convinced that, while the city had ostensibly been districted to prevent *de facto* discrimination against Latino candidates, most voters themselves didn't appear to see the elections in this way – even if the council members were all white.

At the time of redistricting, three of the five council members lived in District 2. Two were pitted against each other in a 2016 at-large race for mayor, with Joe Vinatieri, a Republican attorney at Richard Nixon's old law firm, Bewley, Lassleben, and Miller, beating Owen Newcomer, a Democrat civics professor. The third, Councilmember Bob Henderson, would run for District 2 in 2018. Bob, the wizened lion of Whittier, referred jokingly by some as the "Bobfather," would be vying for his tenth four-year term. Bob had served as the only Democrat on a majority Republican council from 1976 to 1984 when he decided not to run for reelection.

Following the devastating 1987 Whittier Narrows Earth-quake, a conservative, property rights city council had permitted the razing of clapboard bungalows to make way for stucco multi-family homes. This decision altered the older neighbor-hoods' character and brought parking and other quality of life concerns. Bob, a wiry, third-generation insurance salesman, ral-lied residents against the Republicans' pro-growth policies and in opposition to a plan by Chevron to build a large hillside commu-nity on its Whittier holdings. Bob was elected to the council once more in 1990. He would become known, among other things, for preserving the Whittier Hills, protecting them from develop-ment, and converting them into a natural habitat through some nifty legal and financial maneuverings.

By 2016, Bob had gone, to some, from the young, folksy, and pragmatic leader of the insurrectionists to an irascible, stubborn member of the old guard. He had made some decisions that put him at odds with some of his core supporters. After the funding mechanism for the habitat had dried up with the closure of the Puente Hills Landfill (at 700 acres, formerly the largest trash heap in the nation) in 2013, Bob had supported drilling for oil in the Whittier Hills. After the Internet's democratizing influence turned the habitat from sleepy nature backwater to hiker's paradise, with its concomitant nuisances to the communities abutting the trailheads, he had closed off hiking except during work hours, angering local hikers. Despite being a longtime "slow-growther," Bob also backed a 750-unit housing development on about 80 acres of former youth correctional facility called Fred C. Nelles.

Bob had also never fully embraced the local Latino Democrat activists even as Whittier became increasingly Latino (or perhaps they never embraced him). His opposition to liberalizing closing hours at the bars and restaurants of the historic shopping district, Uptown Whittier, put him at odds with young, increasingly cosmopolitan, Latino residents who hoped for a better local nightlife.

I could see that Whittier badly needed to transition from a somewhat isolated backwater to a twenty-first-century town. I felt we needed to cater to young, increasingly affluent Latino residents who wanted more dynamism out of their new hometown – bars, public events, increased investment in arts and entertainment, and so on – and to address vexing social problems like skyrocketing housing prices and homelessness.

Most people I knew agreed the city needed to evolve, and some felt that Bob was standing in the way. I sensed that he was vulnerable. And it had nothing to do with who was occupying the White House or what residents thought about abortion, racism, or gun rights. It had everything to do with the positions Bob had taken on local issues like oil, hiking, and motels.[8] I sensed that whoever could tap into, and give voice to, the dissatisfaction voters felt with the status quo on local matters would have a fighting chance at beating Bob, even though he was still a formidable opponent. A win would mean we could start the process of moving Whittier toward the future, investing more heavily in public transportation and walkability, reducing our overreliance on the automobile, taking measures to make housing affordable for middle-class families, and dealing with homelessness.

So, what are your local issues? Is it the state of the local budget or perhaps the revitalization of a business district? Gang activity? Blight? Traffic? What are some common complaints? What are your elected officials in denial over or ignoring? What must change for your jurisdiction to reach its full potential?

Serving on a board or council isn't just a holding place for future congresspersons. It's for those who take local government seriously, for people with a passion for local issues. Your reward will ultimately be the satisfaction knowing you played a role in making the world just a tiny bit better, not fame, wealth, or accolades.

As we speak, I am trying to relocate a home formerly owned by Richard Nixon to a local park. I'm not much of a Nixon fan, however, he is an important part of our local history. And moving his house, currently in the hands of someone who wants to demolish it to build an office building,[9] would be a boon to local tourism. I will likely never get credit for this endeavor, from the left or right, but it needs to be done.

Before you start your candidacy, ask yourself: what *exactly* will I change if I win my race? What specific issues will voters rally around? Once you know what these are, take the time to research all sides. Understand the issues in more than just a superficial way. Talk to your neighbors. Read the newspaper. Attend council meetings. After all, you can't fix something you don't fully understand.

SUMMARY

^ Voters care first and foremost about their bottom line. That means focusing on local issues, not federal ones.

^ Be pragmatic. Prioritize practical over symbolic goals.

^ You can't fix what you don't get. Know the issues backwards and forward.

^ Only run if you can identify issues worth running for.

CHAPTER 3

ELECTABILITY POLITICS

"Why you?" is probably the most difficult question because you're the least capable of providing the answer. As a fledgling politician, someone has probably told you that you'd make a great candidate, and why not? You're a good person, after all. Isn't the problem that we don't have enough good people in office? It's important to be confident as a politician, but self-exuberance can lead you to see only what you want. And what others see is what decides elections.

Are You Electable?

Traditionally, your job, education, and community ties were your qualifications for office. Having a family was considered more or less a prerequisite. While still true in part, the electorate is thankfully more open-minded about what makes a legitimate candidate than ever before. Today, your life experience and maturity matter more than whether you climbed the corporate ladder or attended the Ivy League. Depending on what you make of your experience, you can learn more from going to jail than Yale.

If you've done, or are doing, something in your life that takes considerable courage and conviction, you can craft a story that will make people want to support your candidacy. If that experience is still years away for you, you may want to reconsider.

They say who you surround yourself with, you become. Your network is a critical aspect of your viability as a candidate. The more extensive and more influential your network, the more formidable of a candidate you will be. That is why the elected ranks are so full of former political staffers and aides. Of course, you don't have to be a political insider to be effective in local politics, but your ability to raise money, to turn out volunteers, and get endorsements matter. This, in turn, depends largely on your network. The people in your network can also give you a good insight into whether you should run. Ask the people you trust to be honest with you about how you present, what you sound like, what you need to work on, and whether or not you're better off running now or later. Don't just pressure them to tell you what you want to hear.

In local races, your ties to the community play a particularly important role. For better or worse, a newcomer to the city just doesn't inspire the same confidence as a longtime resident. That makes sense, as you can't understand a city whose problems you haven't experienced firsthand. People also hold it against you, fairly or not, if you live with your parents.

Well, so far, so good. You have a good story, community ties, and a strong network. Congrats, you're a good candidate – on paper. However, campaigns aren't fought on paper but in real life, in the crucible of an actual campaign where the most significant qualifier is your desire to win. Most obstacles can be overcome depending on how willing you are to sacrifice and grow. If you're ready to stretch yourself and work with blinding intensity, then you'll always have a puncher's chance at succeeding. I would strongly caution you against this being your sole qualification for running, but you can never discount a junkyard dog in the local political arena.

Would You Be a Good Elected Official?

Mike Tyson once said, "If you're not humble, life will visit humbleness on you." This is especially true for politicians. The worst politicians are those who treat politics like a zero-sum game, or any game. Your actions have real-life consequences for people. One of my constituents was a big supporter of mine – until we raised his water bill. Before the increase, he had responded to a Facebook comment of mine that my son has asthma by dropping off a humidifier on my front porch, a kind gesture. After the increase, it was all sarcasm and vitriol directed at me. If he only knew how much it hurt me to increase taxes on people like him living on the margins. A good politician should have drooped shoulders and a furrowed brow. In a word, a good politician *cares*.

Once, when I was a summer intern at the Los Angeles District Attorney's Office, I was invited to play pickup basketball during lunch at the LAPD Academy. The court needed a file down in the courtroom that I had in my car, and a fire drill ensued while I shot hoops. After the commotion died down, a friendly deputy district attorney explained that being a professional is about knowing the difference between the glass and the rubber balls. As a local elected official, you're essentially a juggler. You're constantly juggling at least four balls: the public, the media, staff, and your colleagues.

The public is a glass ball. It can shatter on you at any moment. You need maturity, calmness, buoyancy, bearing, endurance, and tact to interact successfully with members of the public. That means always treating people with respect and courtesy regardless of how they treat you. The other sign when you entered

O'Bannon Hall in Quantico read, "YOU CHOSE US." As an elected official, *you* decided to take responsibility for your jurisdiction, and sometimes this requires that you receive abuse. You must take it in stride. If not, you'll come across as immature and irascible, and your opponents will exploit this weakness. As Chinese military strategist Sun Tzu wrote, "If your opponent is of choleric temper, irritate him."

Your colleagues are another one of those glass balls. It's a complicated relationship, similar to a marriage, except without the option of divorce. Barring a successful recall, you're stuck with each other until at least the next election. Your success is bound up in one another. That means you can grandstand and recriminate them all you want, but unless you can count to three (or whatever number constitutes a majority on your elected body), you won't be effective.

Given that some of your colleagues will be philosophically, and even personally, opposed to you means your qualities must also include creativity, patience, endurance, and a deep sense of purpose. To get your colleagues to vote with you consistently takes earning their respect and trust. It also means finding creative ways to come up with "Godfather offers," that is, offers they can't refuse (because they're too good to turn down). An example is when I found a way to build a homeless shelter by giving my colleagues what they wanted – the ability to once gain enforce our anti-camping laws and park curfew legally.

Can You Handle the Responsibility?

In November of 2019, I passed on the opportunity to run for an open seat in the state assembly. It seemed like a dream job for a politician, with increased prestige, pay, and influence. I wrestled with the decision up until the filing deadline. It was an opening that wouldn't present itself often, and I felt I had the best resume of any potential candidate. I had the support of my family and friends. I also thought I could make a tremendous difference in the state capitol. On the morning of the filing deadline, I put on *Rudy*, the movie about a mediocre but determined athlete who walks on to the Notre Dame football team. It was my dad's favorite movie and encapsulates how I had come to see myself – an everyman who beats the odds to make something of himself. Except my life isn't a movie. Christina had been diagnosed with breast cancer in April 2019 and was still recovering from surgery. And after years of jumping from once accomplishment to the next, I was emotionally exhausted.

Sometimes the timing just isn't right. You might be the best candidate on paper, but if you're struggling with substance abuse, financial challenges, ill health, or emotional issues, you should hold back, get the help you need, and wait for another opportunity. If you have ambition and drive, other chances will inevitably come up. Don't get trapped in the illusion that destiny itself is driving you toward greatness.

Are You the Best Person for the Job?

Whether I was the best person to replace Bob was tough for me to answer before I ran. Although some people were dissatisfied with Bob's choices and others felt the city council had too many long-term incumbents, voters wouldn't abandon someone who had given as much to the community as Bob Henderson for just any opponent. Incumbents, after all, traditionally carry a substantial advantage in their reelection bids. Bob had beaten opponent after opponent, year after year. He hadn't been in office during five decades by accident. The Whittier City Council, moreover, had a reputation for being a careful custodian of the taxpayer's dollar. The city is considered well-run, particularly compared with the scandal-plagued cities of southeast Los Angeles County.[10] The right candidate would be a safe break from the past. As a family man, a professional, and a veteran, I believed I could offer the best balance of change and stability.

Still, I had problems as a candidate. I wasn't a longtime Whittier resident, and Whittierites tend to be small-town exceptionalists who value longstanding ties to the community. At the time of the 2018 election, the three longest-standing councilmembers had a combined tenure of sixty-two years. At the same time, this race was likely going to be different. Dissatisfaction with the status quo meant some level of outsider status could be a plus as long as I could show that I had integrated myself quickly and completely into the community.

Perhaps of greater concern was my limited local network. I had only lived in Whittier for a short time and was just starting to make friends. The best I could hope for was to get the ball rolling with donations from military, law school, and college friends, and hope my initial momentum would bring me into contact with increasingly more people throughout the race.

In a nutshell, while I had a limited network and name recognition, I also had a strong resume, the ability to raise money, and, most important, an ardent desire to win. Based on my experience, I felt confident that I could hold my own as an elected official. I was satisfied I was the best person for the job. This confidence helped keep me going later on when my opponents and their supporters argued strenuously that I most certainly was not.

What about you? Are you ready? Do you have the support you need? Are you hungry to win? Do you have life experience? Are you capable and prepared? If not, what do you need to get yourself to that point? It's normal to have a sense of doubt even if you are, in fact, ready. Still, if you wrestle with these questions and don't feel confident that it's the right time for you, it's okay to sit this one out. There's no shame in it at all.

SUMMARY

^ You don't need to have the traditional qualifications to succeed in the political arena.

^ People won't vote for you if you seem immature or unprepared.

^ Your desire to win is your number one qualification but shouldn't be your only qualification.

^ A good politician cares.

^ You can't succeed in politics if you don't work well with people with whom you disagree.

^ Sometimes, the timing isn't right, and that's okay.

^ Don't talk yourself out of running just because it'll be hard.

CHAPTER 4

PLAN TO WIN

A French poet wrote, "A goal without a plan is just a wish." U.S. Marine General James Mattis was blunter: "Be polite, be professional, but have a plan to kill everybody you meet." While it may seem premature to plan a strategy for a race you haven't decided to enter, this is the exact time to conduct such a preliminary exercise. No plan can, of course, guarantee you a win, but a weak plan can potentially reveal if running will be a waste of time.

Who Are Your Voters?

Even good candidates with the best intentions lose elections because they fail to understand that the point of an election is to get the most votes. Too many candidates go out there and try to get the most votes they can without a solid idea of how many votes they need exactly. They become complacent after receiving some support and undershoot the target. Young candidates are particularly prone to this. Cheaper means of producing and consuming entertainment have driven consumers away from the one-size-fits-all toward the niche. Political campaigns represent something of a countertrend, though. Going niche as a political candidate is a recipe for disaster.

Thus, if you're a knitting champion, you can undoubtedly win a contest for elected office, but only if you can convince a majority, or at least a plurality, of the electorate of your viability as a candidate irrespective of your particular identity. There just aren't enough professional knitters to support such a candidate just as there weren't enough French-surnamed Latinos to earn me a win. Unfortunately, modern technology seats us comfortably inside an echo chamber, which continually reinforces the idea that our particular tribe is destined for electoral victory. If you're repeatedly told how our country's future rests upon the election of more knitters, you might start to believe you're destined to win because you're such a good knitter. And relying on fate to carry you to victory isn't a winning strategy; it's a political death sentence. While people do generally like to identify with their politicians, they mostly just vote with their wallets at the local level.

While it's true that declining voter participation means you need a lower and lower number of voters to mount a successful bid for office, it's just not enough to galvanize a passionate but numerically insignificant subset of the population. The local electorate is simply too dynamic for numerical minorities to win elections. Majorities can and will form to reject perceived attempts at a takeover by a fraction of the electorate.

That's not to say identity is irrelevant. If you can appeal to a readily discernible group of voters, whether through political, gender, or ethnic affinity, then the race is handicapped in your favor. But you can't rely exclusively on identity. I remember, for instance, thinking, "Well, I'm the only Latino," until that ceased being the case. Then I thought, "At least I'm the only person with young kids," until that was no longer true. Finally, I thought, "Still, I'm the only veteran." Next thing I knew, a guy married to a vet was running against me.

Any candidate, irrespective of what tribe they affiliate with, will need to identify *multiple* distinct voting blocs – whether organized by voter propensity, age, dwelling type, ethnicity, affluence, political affiliation, or some other identifying feature – to have a reasonable chance to gain an electoral victory. You must get an accurate idea of whom exactly you must appeal to in order to win. Your strategy and efforts stem from this analysis.

Having immersed myself in Whittier politics in the years following my honorable discharge from the Marine Corps, I became convinced that Bob no longer enjoyed widespread support. He was relying on an electorate comprised of aging white center-left voters who had supported and benefited from his post-quake protectionist policies, which had lifted their home values. Frankly, there just weren't enough of these voters left. They had either aged out or moved away. I felt confident I could beat him one-on-one. And then Irella Perez entered the race.

Irella won election to the Whittier City School District Board of Education in 2011. A single mother of five, Irella is a force of nature with her intense stare, perfectly coiffed hair, and pastel pantsuits. She has a dignified air, enhanced by her sonorous Nicaraguan accent. She can be incredibly nice but can also be somewhat intimidating.

Named after Cinderella, Perez had a Cinderella past in some ways. During the Nicaraguan Civil War, Irella and her family fled to America where her parents worked menial jobs. Irella, by any measure, did admirably for herself in the U.S., obtaining a doctorate and rising up the ranks to become the superintendent of a high school district. As superintendent, Irella was dismissed after only a few months. (Irella later sued the school district and won).11 As a city commissioner, an elected school board member, and a tenacious campaigner, she would be a formidable opponent in spite of her recent dismissal. Although my mother and father were also Latin American immigrants, I knew that, because of my gender and my French last name, I'd have a tough time with voters who wanted to kick the whites off the council, and also with voters who preferred a woman.

Usually, there would also have been a Republican in the race. However, it appeared that the Republican establishment would back Bob. That meant my coalition would, by necessity, consist of Democrats disaffected due to Bob's recent policy stances, Republicans who might vote for a Democrat military veteran in a nonpartisan race, and liberal Democrats who might be turned off by Irella's recent publicity. I also banked on the hypothesis that Latino voters are not a monolithic group and would support a candidate without a Spanish surname. Still, I knew we would have to thread the needle to win.

Outside observers thought I was crazy to even think of challenging Bob, much less Irella. Conventional wisdom told them there was simply too little electorate left to go around. One older, white liberal activist told me, "Henry, you should really consider dropping out. With you not being a woman or having a Spanish last name, you couldn't possibly do better than third place." This was apparently his idea of racial and gender equality. Fortunately, conventional wisdom is only right most of the time. While they were correct that there was little chance a conventional Democrat could win a race like this, I didn't employ a conventional strategy. Without a Republican candidate, and with this technically being a nonpartisan race, I planned to appeal to moderate Democrats,

Republicans, and young liberals. And the reality was, in a local election, concepts of left, right, and center aren't nearly as important or clear-cut.

The syllogism that without knowing whom you must win over, you can't win them over should be self-evident by now. It's true even if you have the most money, the best intentions, and the most robust qualifications. You must know who must vote for you. This is true whether you are, like I was, a Democrat running against two other Democrats or whether you are a Democrat running against a Republican or vice versa. You have to ask yourself: Which coalition of demographic groups are amenable to voting for me, and do I have a decent shot at winning them over to my side? That's just the first step, though. To make this information actionable, you must next determine just how many voters you need to win over.

How Many Votes Do You Need?

Besides knowing what types of voters that you need, you must also understand how many individual votes it takes to win. These are two distinct undertakings. The latter is a statistical analysis, while the former is a demographic one. This isn't a discovery of mine. Candidates are typically taught to research historical election results to determine how many votes, the so-called "magic number," are necessary to win the race and work backward from that statistic to develop a campaign strategy.

Before officially entering the race, I attempted to find our magic number by requesting voter data from the county registrar recorder. It was guesswork to a degree because Bob had only run under the former at-large, citywide election system, and Irella had run in a district that encompassed most, but not all, of District 2. Still, comparing apples to oranges is better than flying blind (to mix metaphors).

By requesting maps and results by precinct, I was more or less able to piece together what Bob's support looked like in the district. To give you an idea of what this analysis looks like, below is a paraphrased email that I circulated to my team (more on them later). For context, there are about 20,000 residents and around 12,000 registered voters in District 2.

Total votes for Bob have gone from 4,071 in 2002 to 4,533 in 2010, and 3,555 in 2014, confirming that Bob's support is waning.

As a proportion of the overall vote, Bob's vote-by-mail numbers increased from 2010 to 2014. In 2010, it was 724 voters at the poll versus 802 mailed-in. In 2014, however, it was 434 at the polls versus 693 vote-by-mail. This tells me we have to make a hard run at absentee voters from the jump and definitely once ballots can be mailed.

I expected Bob to pull significantly from voters outside the district, but he's actually drawn about a third of his votes from the district. He draws well in precincts 6, 8, and 12/15, College Hills, North Whittier Hills, and Uptown East/West, respectively. These are the higher propensity voting precincts.

By doing this analysis, I was able to confirm my hypothesis that support had been waning for Bob, particularly among poll voters (who tend to be younger and non-white in this area. This example should give you an idea of why you need to look at the numbers closely. I assumed Bob had stayed in power because he had strong support outside his home district. That wasn't actually the case. Bob was doing better in District 2 than elsewhere, likely thanks to older, more affluent voters in these neighborhoods. While beatable, he wouldn't be a walkover.

Irella's potential performance was trickier to nail down. Her school board district consisted of parts of east Whittier that were outside of Council District 2 and would thus not be voting in our election, and parts of unincorporated Los Angeles County adjacent to the City of Whittier. Still, she was the lead vote-getter in 2011, obtaining 1,043 votes, in a race that included another candidate with the same last name, Cecilia Perez. Irella was going to be a formidable adversary.

Now that I understood my opponents' past performances, I began to make educated guesses about voter turnout and our opponents' likely performance based on past vote tallies. Here's another email to sum up:

> Bob obtained 1,060 votes from District 2 precincts in 2014 out of a total of 3,436 votes citywide, or 15.85% voter turnout. Assuming slightly higher turnout due to districting, we can conservatively assume there will be 3,600 votes at play in District 2. Bob may receive a slight boost from increased turnout, but his favorability has suffered since 2014 and the sentiment that he has

been around too long has increased. Irella's potential performance is more difficult to gauge. 2011 was before her negative press and it was also a much lower turnout race. Being charitable, we can give her 1,043 votes. That leaves 1,497 votes for the taking.

Essentially, I thought Bob and Irella would each get about a thousand votes and that we would need at least a thousand to compete and 1,200 to be safe. As you can see, arriving at a magic number is an inexact science, but it can help guide your efforts. Knowing how many votes I needed, I built a ground game to get them. It helped me set daily and weekly benchmarks for doors to hit, which kept me focused on my target throughout the race. That is no small matter given how much anxiety a drawn-out local race can produce considering the lack of polling data available to local candidates (due to the expense).

Ultimately, 2,851 votes were cast in District 2, short of what I had expected. We ended up getting 1,095 votes to Bob's 982 and Irella's 546. Voter turnout increased from the low teens to nearly a quarter of registered voters but not quite as much as we had expected. Still, my assessment wasn't too far off from what transpired.

Failing to crunch your magic number, particularly when you're facing opponents with a long history of elections, is like going into a knife fight in the dark. You might somehow win, but only if you're lucky, and even then, you're probably going to be a bloody mess in the end. It's useful to know what you're up against and how far you have to come from behind. In my case, the task was to go from a virtual unknown to a serious contender in four short months. And with a little number crunching, I set the stage for it to happen.

One final word of caution: take your numbers as they are. Don't make the mistake of using magical thinking in your calculations. That means you shouldn't expect a blue wave or a red wave to dramatically increase voter turnout in a way that will give you the extra votes you need.[12] As they say in business, "past performance is the best indicator of future success." You also shouldn't expect people to fall so deeply in love with you as a candidate that those who have never voted before will suddenly rush to their neighborhood polling center to support you. As my consultant frequently reminded me, "You're not Obama." Rare in the extreme is the politician who can turn out apathetic voters. That doesn't mean you can't increase the size of the voting electorate by some incremental amount. However, there is simply only so much time, money, and volunteers available to even the best local candidate to earn a substantial increase in the number of voters. You're more or less stuck with your pool of voters and must develop a strategy to win over as much of this electorate as you can while staying true to your values.

Don't think you have to be a math whiz to pull this analysis off, by the way. Although I'm financially literate and you should be too, I frankly don't remember how to do long division anymore. If breaking out a calculator gives you the willies, ask a friend to help you. Hire a political consultant for the limited purpose of undertaking this analysis if need be. Trust me. It's worth the time, effort, and heartache as it's better to lose on paper, before committing yourselves and others to such a significant endeavor, than to lose in real life.

SUMMARY

^ You can't win without a plan. Start by figuring out how many votes you need to succeed.

^ Keep in mind that your race is just one of many on the ballot.

^ Don't anticipate increased voter turnout. Let past participation be your guide.

^ Being a niche candidate is a recipe for failure. Strive for a broad coalition.

^ Concepts of liberal, conservative, and moderate become muddled in local, nonpartisan races.

RESOURCES

For instructions on how to source demographic information and other useful tools, visit authorhenrybouchot.com.

CHAPTER 5

STRATEGERY

Campaign marketing and communications efforts are empty unless you hold a competitive advantage over your adversaries. You can't win an election without a competitive advantage. A competitive advantage isn't merely in your head. It's not just a mindset. Earnestness, thus, isn't a competitive advantage. A competitive advantage isn't just something you *have*, either. Money, supporters, a good resume, or name recognition aren't enough to beat the best candidates. A competitive advantage is a strength that you put into action. It can, for example, be intelligence, eloquence, or resourcefulness. My competitive advantage, for example, was my tenaciousness.

Know Yourself

Throughout my life, I've rarely been the biggest, fastest, or the strongest. Perseverance is my calling card. I passed the California bar exam while working full-time in the Marines because I started studying a year before the exam, while deployed to Afghanistan, and after returning, listening to exam prep tapes while exercising and writing out practice essays after work and during weekends. This trait is a family inheritance. I remember my dad telling me how he quit smoking *and* drinking cold turkey and about the time he ran laps for weeks, preparing in secret before challenging a guy to a sprint who had embarrassed him in a foot race.

Given my single-mindedness, I knew adopting a strategy relying on pace and endurance would be to my strategic advantage. This strategy was based on maneuver warfare doctrine, a philosophy the Marines adapted from the Germans in the First World War, which emphasizes decentralized command and advocates defeating your enemy by incapacitating their decision-making through shock and disruption. For me, this meant building up my strength surreptitiously over many months, and then, once my plan was in place, relentlessly pushing the offensive, staying one step ahead of my opponents at all times. It meant putting them, as they say in the Corps, "in the horns of a dilemma." My goal would be to make my opponents react to my moves, decisions, and strategy rather than adapting to theirs. And my competitive advantage made me capable of executing this strategy since I was prepared for the months of grinding preparations it would take.

Your strategy can be whatever fits your style, experience, and preference. I'm not advocating for a no holds barred approach where you treat campaigning like war. What I'm recommending is that you identify an overarching game plan based on one of your core strengths. Otherwise, your campaign will be reactive, shifting according to the day's prevailing whims. A lack of strategic focus will only lead you into rabbit holes as you follow your opponent's lead, responding to someone else's strategy rather than imposing your own.

How exactly do you identify your competitive advantage? Well, what are your skills? What makes you special? If you have experience as an actor, as Ronald Reagan did, perhaps your competitive advantage lies in your ability to incorporate histrionics into your strategy. Maybe you're a great debater. You might challenge your opponent to a series of debates as Abraham Lincoln did in his Senate race against Stephen Douglas. If you're adept at research and detail-oriented work, you might put together a file on your opponent so damaging that their endorsers will run for the hills as "tricky" Dick Nixon undoubtedly did. The point is you must find something you're good at because your strength is unique to you and decide how you can leverage it in a way that puts your opponents at a disadvantage.

Know Your Adversaries

If "know thyself" is the first commandment of strategic campaigning, "know thine enemy" is the second. Understanding your opponent is more than just making a list of strengths and weaknesses. The Marine Corps has another concept called "critical vulnerabilities" that's instructive. These are key weaknesses that, if exploited, will sow failure within your enemy. Ask yourself what their critical vulnerabilities are and how you can take advantage of them as you develop your strategy.

I sometimes joke that I knew Bob better than he knew himself by the end of the campaign. One of the fortunate aspects of running against a longtime incumbent such as Bob was that his career had been cataloged in rich detail in local publications like the *Whittier Daily News*. An oral history he provided to the local library regarding his role in protecting the Whittier Hills was a treasure trove for me. I came to believe that he was a man who was heavily invested in his legacy. That had led him to increasingly overlook the day-to-day, street-level concerns of his constituents in favor of large, legacy-shaping projects, making him appear increasingly out of touch. He was also sometimes just plain cranky, lecturing people from the dais. Since I couldn't expect to beat him by comparing resumes, I decided to show the voters just how much more I cared about their neighborhoods through my actions as a candidate.

Irella hadn't received anywhere near the same amount of media coverage as Bob had, but there was enough information out there for me to assess her. Since we ran in similar circles, I also had greater access to her contemporaries than I did with Bob. Plus, with the robust California Public Records Act at my side, I could obtain information that was public but not widely available like her termination letter from her previous job.

Irella's most significant weaknesses was her lack of expertise in municipal government. While she could speak coherently on education, she struggled to inspire similar confidence in her grasp of municipal affairs, often reading from a script. I planned to exploit this vulnerability of hers through my preparations.

Don't lose hope if there are other qualified candidates in your race. A good rival can be indispensable. A strong opponent keeps you on your toes, motivated and sharp. Rivalry can bring out your creativity and force you to think two steps ahead. Embrace the competition. In this sense, Irella and Bob helped make me a winner. Their presence in the race motivated me to grow, improve, and develop myself into the type of candidate that would surface to the top and gain the respect and trust of voters.

You should, therefore, avoid vilifying your rivals and their supporters. There's a certain hysteria that inflicts even the most reasonable candidates, and it can become severe the closer you get to the election. Worrying that people are out to get you, that you can't even trust your supporters, or feeling like you can't beat your opponent no matter what you do is the perfect recipe for misery and failure. Every opponent has weaknesses. Find them and make them work for you.

Know Your Business

Running for office isn't a mere popularity contest. Too many well-meaning candidates go into local politics expecting that the public will rush to their side and, like in *Rudy*, carry them on their shoulders to victory. It just doesn't happen that way. People are busy and local elections are more often than not just an afterthought as they manage lives crowded with work, commutes, and family obligations.

One of my opponents, Eric Leckey, a fringe candidate who jumped in the race just before the filing deadline, was an articulate, humorous family man. He designed his own lawn signs and handouts and consistently knocked on doors throughout the district, often with his two daughters in tow. Eric captivated the audience during debates with a breathless, slapstick style. In the end, he received a mere 78 votes. While Eric likely fared well at the doors he was able to hit, he didn't scale his operations in a way that would put him in front of enough voters to win.

Eric portrayed himself as an entrepreneur and as a business turnaround artist, touting his success with multimillion-dollar companies. Eric is in the wine industry and has a flair for salesmanship (he even writes pulp noir fiction). Sales, however, are only one aspect of running for office. To become a great candidate, you must achieve basic competence in the full suite of business skills, including accounting, finance, marketing, operations, sales, management, and strategy. Doing so will allow you to create the scale you need to reach thousands of voters with just a small team and limited resources.

When I was a Captain in the Marine Corps, I served as a prosecutor. My boss was a former helicopter pilot who had been injured in a training accident, literally pulling himself from the fiery crash shortly before the helicopter became engulfed in flames. He was severely burned and lost several fingers on one hand. He recovered, earned a law degree, and became a judge advocate. He was fiercely competitive, turning games of ultimate Frisbee into trench warfare. You would expect advice from a man like that to center around perseverance and "working harder than your opponent." Instead, his key takeaway was to be "brilliant in the basics." In the Marines, they say "slow is smooth and smooth is fast" when referring to the best approach for rifle marksmanship. It's the equivalent to the tortoise's approach versus the hare. Avoid getting distracted by flash and unfocused activity and develop a basic brilliance across the spectrum of campaign functions.

While running for office is radically different from holding office, running a campaign is something of a barometer for voters on your qualifications. The public wants you to *show*, not just *tell* them that you're the right choice. The best way to do this is by running a clean, well-oiled, professional campaign free from major missteps or scandals. Treat your campaign like a successful startup business, and you'll make a formidable opponent in any local race.

SUMMARY

^ A strategic advantage is not just something you have. It's something you do.

^ Your strategic advantage should be tailored to your particular strengths as well as your opponent's weaknesses.

^ Embrace competition. It strengthens you.

^ Campaigning is like running a startup. Master this business and you'll have a shot at winning almost any race.

RESOURCES

For a reading list on business and military strategy, a sample public records act request letter, and more check out authorhenrybouchot.com.

PART II

PRE-CAMPAIGN

"Ambition must be used to benefit the state; else it is wrong,
and God must strike it from this earth."
– SOPHOCLES

CHAPTER 6

DO AS I SAY

So, you've decided that running for office is for you and no one can convince you otherwise. You know why you're running, who you're running against, and how you plan to win. Time to get on the ballot, right? Maybe, or maybe not. Perhaps you should if you have name recognition, party operative cred, or if you ran the last time and are the presumptive favorite this time. If so, you may want to skip ahead to Part III, the campaign section. If buying this book was your first step on the road toward becoming a politician, keep reading.

★

Earlier, I urged you to run for the right reasons. What happens, though, if you've already gone off the rails? What if you're running because you're dissatisfied with your career or because code enforcement made you rip up your prized lawn? What if you lost a previous race badly and want payback? Is there still hope for you?

For me, running for office stemmed from a series of painful experiences that started with a deployment to Afghanistan and ended with me quitting my job. In between was the death of my father. After four years in the Marines, I'd taken a position as an aide to the Mayor of Los Angeles and moved to Whittier for good. I was hired to manage government public safety contracts and, so

I thought, to participate in developing policing policy. I was quickly disappointed by civilian work. Before joining the mayor's office, I was advising generals and providing direct input on drone strikes. I had literally put men in jail with the stroke of a pen. At the mayor's office, my boss wanted to look over my emails before I sent them.

I had gone from a place of tremendous responsibility, autonomy, and even prestige to one of micromanagement, mundaneness, and shut-up-and-color. I felt like I was drowning. I begged for the opportunity to take on meaningful work, extra work even. My drive, however, was met with suspicion. In the Marine Corps, ambition, enthusiasm, and loyalty to the institution are drivers of success. In Los Angeles politics, dedication to the boss, patience, face time, and waiting your turn were the marks of a team player. Having witnessed innocent civilians die in Afghanistan due to incompetence and overzealousness, my distrust of authority was severe. My loyalty was to constituents only, not any particular politician, and definitely not some bureaucrat. In retrospect, the mayor's office simply wasn't a good fit for me.

Against this backdrop, my desire to break into Whittier politics was both an outlet for my career frustrations and an escape from combat trauma.[13] It was a way for me to transcend painful experiences by doing some good in the world. What any sane person might have seen as an impossible challenge – coming into a new city and taking down a revered incumbent councilman – I saw as the perfect release. Politics offered me the allure of significant responsibility without direct supervision and a chance to redo my Afghanistan experience, subverting authority to make the world right again.

What ensued was a haphazard series of efforts that led me from a frustrated employee to a local activist and upstart politician. I wouldn't recommend such an effort to you. However, I'll share this story with you as a way to show that even those who have a wayward start can find their way in the world of local politics.

In contrast to my naked, blunted efforts at rising in Los Angeles politics, my initial steps in Whittier were careful and measured. The last thing I wanted to do was to start shouting my intentions for holding elected office from the rooftops after being stymied at the City of Los Angeles.

It started at *La Pescadora*, a Mexican surf-and-turf restaurant with a nightclub-style red-velvet rope at the entrance. It was the fall of 2015, about thirty months before my race. My college friend Daniel Malignaggi had agreed to meet me there with the same idea in mind. "Are you thinking what I'm thinking?" (Jinx). We'd both recently moved to and bought homes in Whittier, completing the upward-bound, eastward trek from East Los Angeles. Aside from a few political science classes under our belts, we were political newbies. We knew, though, that politics is where you could make a real difference.

The first district elections in Whittier were still a few months away, but we knew only what we'd read in the newspapers: Whittier had been recently broken up into council districts, and someone with enough chutzpah might finally break up the good old boys' club. It felt audacious and even conspiratorial to be asking whether a total unknown like me could successfully break into the bastion of conservatism and establishment politics that was Whittier.

Daniel and I hoped to get me noticed by taking a stance on an important issue. That issue seemed to come when in November of

2015, plastic bags containing KKK propaganda and, oddly enough, Tootsie Rolls, showed up for the second time that year on Whittier doors.[14]

The first time, in June of 2015, the Whittier Latino Coalition, a group of Democrat Latino activists, had called a press conference urging the Whittier Police Department to investigate.[15] The second time around, there had been no press conference. The council took no stand on either occasion. I drafted a letter to the editor of the *Whittier Daily News* urging the council to "issue a formal resolution disavowing these actions and committing to specific measures to foster a renewed sense of diversity and camaraderie" in Whittier.[16] No one seemed to notice, however, including the council.

This was a good learning lesson for me. It indicated that Whittier actually enjoys relatively peaceful race relations. While isolated racial animus does exist, Whittier isn't a hotbed for racial strife. More importantly, it taught me that there would be no shortcuts to becoming a political insider.

With my first effort at gaining exposure going nowhere, I turned my attention to electoral politics. With the District 1 election in Whittier only a few months away, I decided I might have better luck helping someone else get elected.

The Districts 1 and 3 elections in Whittier were scheduled for April (Whittier is one of Southern California's few remaining cities to hold its elections off the November cycle). District 3 consists of wealthy Friendly Hills and is a Republican stronghold. Perhaps because of this, no one signed up to run against incumbent Cathy Warner, a dental hygienist who was first elected in 2004. With the mayor's race pitting two established councilmen, Republican Joe Vinatieri and Democrat Owen Newcomer, each residing in

District 2, the only contested race featuring a non-establishment candidate that year would be District 1.

Whittier has long been a Republican town (a supporter of mine in her seventies describes a time when the polling locations had six booths for Republicans and one for Democrats). The only time Whittier was in the hands of Democrats was during the immediate post-earthquake years (1992 to 2004) when Democrats held as many as five council seats. On the surface, these Democrats were relatively leftist, bent on preserving the natural environment from corporate encroachment. Even still, there was a conservative streak to them. While they opposed the strict property-rights focus of the Republicans, they ultimately shared cultural and ethnic ties with their conservative counterparts. Mostly white, lifelong Whittierites, they were fiscal conservatives and social moderates.

There had never been a Latino Democrat on the city council even though this had become the largest voting bloc. Vic Lopez, a high school football coach and a Republican, had been the only Latino ever elected to Whittier's council. He served from 1978 to 1990, including two terms as mayor. The District 1 election would be the first opportunity to elect a Latino Democrat to the council. For the Latino activists of the Whittier Latino Coalition and other Latino activist groups, the nuances of the various council members' political ideologies weren't as important as the fact that they were all white. Several local Latino activists joined forces with civil rights attorneys from the Mexican American Legal Defense and Educational Fund (MALDEF). They sued to break Whittier into districts, arguing that at-large elections *de facto* discriminated against the Latino population since minorities rarely won citywide races.

Rather than lose in court, the city formulated its own redistricting plan, known as Measure W (not to be confused with the 2020 local sales tax measure). Using a process known as "packing," the council drew the new districts in a way that maintained the traditional balance of power. They did this by creating an at-large mayor, one heavily Latino district, District 1, and one affluent district, District 3. Friendly Hills, a hilly community near the Friendly Hills Country Club, which has homes rivaling Brentwood and Bel-Air, is in District 3. This district is also the whitest and most conservative district. By contrast, District 1 is working-class, Latino (84% as of 2016), and Democratic.

Louis Reyes, a local Democrat political consultant and a member of the Whittier Latino Coalition, was expected to be the District 1 candidate for the Latino Democrats. However, he declined to run for personal reasons and without designating a successor. (Louis later ran unsuccessfully for mayor in 2020).

At the eleventh hour, a virtually unknown Democrat named Josue Alvarado entered the race, self-funding his campaign with an $8,000 loan. My first time attending a meeting of the Whittier Latino Coalition happened to coincide with him seeking their endorsement. It was a rare drizzly February day in Southern California. About a dozen of us had met in the basement of the massive, baby blue rectangular First Christian church on the corner of Greenleaf and Hadley. Soft-spoken and wearing a brown suit, Josue struck me more like an evangelical youth minister than a politician. Josue had apparently run unsuccessfully for school board in South Whittier. He had also been student body president at nearby Rio Hondo Community College. However, Josue was clearly still adjusting to his newfound role as a liberal savior.

Despite some reservations, the progressives seemed grateful to have someone in the race at all. The Republicans were running an adjunct professor named David Gonzalez. A third candidate, a transgender security guard named Rebecca Canales, who was running under her assigned name of Robert, was expected to place third.

Negative mailers, presumably sent by the Gonzalez camp, revealed that Josue had three misdemeanors on his record. He pled guilty in separate incidents in 2001 to credit card fraud and to taking part in a public fight. In June 2003, he plead guilty to spousal abuse. Josue and his supporters fended off the attacks as smear efforts while also effectively laying the blame at the victim's hands in the spousal abuse case. This was before the #MeToo movement. It's hard to imagine a male politician winning today given such accusations. It goes to show how badly the long shut-out Latino Democrat activists wanted to claim a council seat from the Republicans.

By that point, I had already committed to supporting Josue. Because I didn't live in District 1, I didn't receive the mailers, hearing about them secondhand from people who painted them as libelous. Josue had called me mid-race to ask if I would help him canvass (he received my contact info from the sign-in sheet at the Latino Coalition meeting). He'd gained some ground in the intervening period, picking up supporters and growing in confidence. Apparently, the local Democrat representatives in the state legislature had thrown their support behind him too. Josue and I walked the district together with my toddler in tow. When Josue came over a few days later to return my jacket, which I had left in his car, he had taken an interest in me. He'd even apparently read my letter to the editor.

Josue ultimately won, receiving forty-eight percent of the vote to forty-two percent for Gonzalez and ten percent for Canales.[17] We were exultant on election night as we gathered in a dark, cavernous local nightclub named Sage, which for whatever reason, doubles as the go-to meeting place for local Democratic clubs. Our exuberance grew as the night wore on, and the results came in. People hugged, cheered, and toasted when it became evident Josue would win.

As a candidate for local office, there's such a limited base of support, particularly early on in a race, that those who come out and put in the time to help – whether by knocking on doors, making phone calls, or providing money – are noticed and appreciated. At least half a dozen people at Josue's election night party would run for office in the ensuing years, some successfully. Campaigns can also help lay the groundwork for your own run. Joining political races helps build your network but also, critically, boosts your confidence. This is no small matter. You can compete with the best practices, but you can't win without believing in yourself. Armed with newfound confidence and connections, I was now poised to run myself, or so I thought.

★

As I said before, there are no shortcuts for getting elected to local office. By all means, build a network and get endorsements where you can. However, beware of the allure of getting swept into office on someone else's coattails. This is politics. Until proven otherwise, assume that everyone's in it for themselves and trust only in what you have earned the hard way.

Unfortunately, I failed to heed my own advice. I put myself in an awkward position by telling Josue a month following his election that I was interested in running for District 2 in 2018. I had invited him over one Friday evening to ask for his support. In my head, I pictured Josue voicing his enthusiastic confidence and supporting my run by being a mentor, a confidante, a benefactor even. Josue, however, wanted significant control over my campaign, it quickly became apparent, something I wasn't prepared to hand over. Josue must have seen me as more of an adversary than an ally, as a threat to his aspirations for higher office. (He ultimately ran unsuccessfully for state assembly in 2020, placing fourth and giving up his council seat).[18]

One of my reasons for writing this book is to demystify the process of running to give politically inclined neophytes the courage to take the plunge into local politics. Trusting people and those who lack confidence are often inclined to attach themselves to established politicians. My advice is to trust in yourself, first and foremost. You either have what it takes to run for office successfully or not. Putting your fate in the hands of someone else is only doing you a disservice. You become used to taking orders instead of giving them. Taking orders, however, is poor training for serving on a council. You also deprive the public of getting to know you in an unfiltered, authentic way. Of course, you don't always see a person for who they are right off, and I continued to put my faith in Josue, although only for a time. In the end, I wasn't about to be somebody's flunky. No way, Josue.

SUMMARY

- ^ There are no shortcuts to becoming an elected official.
- ^ As a politician, you must be a chameleon. Wait to show your true colors until you fully understand the environment, lest a predator eats you.
- ^ Supporting candidates is a great way to network and build up your confidence but chose carefully.
- ^ Don't ride someone else's coattails. You either have what it takes or you don't.

CHAPTER 7

DO IT YOURSELF

A better approach than seeking patronage is to make yourself a contender by building a portfolio of local activism based on your own interests and expertise. Ideally, your pre-campaign self should be a scaled-down version of what you'll be like as an elected official. My problem, as I came to find, was that I forgot the scaled-down part. As a law school friend of mine once told me, "You can do everything you want. You just can't do it all at once."

Looking back, I was involved in an insane amount of activities. In April of 2016, I got a new job at a legal aid nonprofit working with homeless vets. My new supervisor stressed the importance of work-life balance. The energy and momentum that came from participating in the victorious District 1 election, however, launched me into something of a shadow campaign (since I hadn't publicly announced my intentions to run yet). I was effectively running for office over a year early. Considering that I was also attending grad school on weekends while raising two children under three, I had taken on a staggering amount of work.

Perhaps the worst example of my over-exuberance was when I gave a public presentation on Uptown's revitalization on my wedding anniversary, which fell on a weekday. While Christina gave me her blessing (we planned to celebrate on the weekend), I can only imagine how neglected she must have felt. I had learned of the Friends of Uptown from an email and decided to check them out. Rather than reject my overtures as the bombast of a wannabe candidate for office, they apparently saw me as a fresh voice for the Uptown merchants.

On the day of the presentation, two dozen or so residents and business owners piled into a small, dark rectangular walkup DJ bar called Spin Lounge. The part-owner, Jesse, a realtor, hadn't closed shop, so patrons were talking loudly at the bar. As soon as I stopped talking, Rebecca, a local philanthropist who lives in an oil-era mansion adorned with original Diego Rivera paintings,[19] peppered me with questions. Rebecca ripped into me and my lovely vision for Uptown, taking her vendetta against the dollar stores, the loiterers, and the absentee landlords up with me.

I also joined the American Legion, hoping to connect with fellow veterans. I ran a phone-banking event at my house during the run-up to the presidential election and interviewed for the local Boys and Girls Club's board of directors. I invited an author to speak at City Hall for Veterans Day (the asking price was too high). I organized a community meeting on policing. I toured a local shelter and the local museum. I attended meet-and-greets for various political candidates. I even skipped work to go to the annual State of the City presentation. No local event or meeting was too unimportant for me. I even popped up at community meetings on trash hauling.

I was like a sponge. I wanted to know anything and everything about local politics. I contacted the mayors of South Gate (Jorge Morales) and West Hollywood (Lindsey Horvath), whom I had met through professional contacts, and learned about their own campaigns. I canvassed in Pacoima for Monica Rodriguez, a former colleague, who was running for the Los Angeles City Council.

This behavior, you probably guessed it, led to burnout. In December 2016, Christina and I were invited to ride in the local Christmas parade with the Whittier Historic Neighborhood Association. Toddlers and infants being what they are, we were late, and I grew utterly frustrated. More than anything, I realized I was upset with myself for getting so carried away. What should've been a lovely event had me fuming as I walked to the starting line, wondering whether running for office was a good idea at all.

That Christmas, while stuck in the doldrums of winter in Connecticut with Christina's family, I sank into a deep funk. I was just plain low, anxious, gloomy, and morose. With Whittier thousands of miles to the west, I could no longer escape my problems by preparing for the campaign. I was distraught over the casualties we had inflicted in Afghanistan. I was grieving my father. Raising two kids, going to grad school, holding down a full-time job, and running for political office had only exacerbated what was already a challenging situation. For the first time in my life, I couldn't overcome obstacles by merely working harder. I had to find a new way.

★

I began by taking a hard look at my lifestyle. I scaled down, slowed down, and quit anything that didn't pay the bills. I stopped going to nearly all of the myriad neighborhood events. I no longer brought up running with my friends. I quit organizing community meetings. I cut out any vexatious person or organization causing me to be unavailable to my loved ones. For all intents and purposes, I put the campaign on pause. I began to read and exercise again. I started going to therapy.

As I said earlier, you need to run for the right reason. I realized my reason at the time was to run away from my problems. My family life and my mental health were all the worse for doing so. Cicero, the Roman statesman, remarked that almost every destructive rumor that makes its way to the public arena begins among family and friends. If I was going to run successfully for office, I first had to secure the home front. That meant getting my priorities straight and taking better care of myself and my family.

Running for local office is, above all, an experience. You can have the best tactics, the most money, and the most experienced advisors. Still, you won't succeed, and you won't survive in politics if you don't take care of yourself. That means understanding your true motivations and changing them if they're not righteous and life-affirming. In the novel *The Power of One*, Bryce Courtenay writes, "First with the head and then with the heart." Well, for me, it should have been more like first with the heart and then with the head. I learned the hard way that the drive for power and accomplishment (the head) could only get me so far. I needed to dig deep and get right with myself (the heart) before running.

★

While there are perils to getting over-involved, you still need to make a name for yourself. This isn't like running for Congress or governor, where your status as a powerful businessperson or celebrity can put you in the running. You need to get involved somewhere. The trick is picking right.

How you choose to get involved will depend on your particular situation. If you're a community activist, you'll be intimately familiar with one or more issues and have a network of people to lean on. Even then, you'll want to avoid being narrowly defined by a single issue. While it's tempting to hope one issue will sweep you into power, the reality is local residents are rarely single-issue voters.

For example, a slate of three Whittier candidates ran unsuccessfully in 2012 to unseat the three incumbents who had voted to explore drilling for oil in the Whittier Hills. Even the unpopular choice to support oil drilling failed to capture more than a sliver of the city's voting bloc. The upstarts lost decisively.[20] While it's advisable to champion causes to raise your profile, you should also diversify your activities to come off as a well-rounded, multi-faceted candidate. In short, don't let yourself be pigeonholed.

Your membership in community organizations, like your support for causes, should tell a story about you. Avoid joining just any club or, worse, every local group. Irella took that approach, and it backfired on her. She sent out a flyer during my race with a list of two-dozen or so organizations to which she ostensibly belonged. Voters questioned, perhaps understandably, just how deep her commitment to that many organizations could really be.

Be strategic about the groups you join. You might be a master knitter but joining the local knitting group, the woodworkers, or the ornithological society isn't likely to help your run for office. Take the time to subscribe to the local newspaper. Watch local city council meetings (not just the public comment portion at the beginning). Get an idea of the most critical issues and the key players. From there, choose those groups that align themselves with your politics and policy goals.

Eventually, I chose to be a member of just a handful of groups. I joined the Whittier Historic Neighborhood Association because Christina and I lived in a historic home. Also, the preservation of historic homes is an important issue to voters in my district. I started a Neighborhood Watch on my block because I felt it was essential to take an active role in my neighborhood's safety. I became a founding member of the Rio Hondo Democratic Club, which proved helpful in getting me the nod from the Los Angeles County Democratic Party. I accepted an invitation to join a local youth nonprofit board. Just joining groups isn't enough, though. The last thing people want from a potential councilmember is dead weight. Put your energy behind a handful of worthwhile efforts that lift up the community. Campaigns are at their best when they tap into a sense of belonging. In this sense, community organizing is useful preparation for campaigning. Voters don't want you to wait until you're elected to make a difference locally. Rather than hitching your wagon to an established politician or group, consider circulating a petition or encouraging your neighbors to speak at a council meeting on a specific topic.

Sometimes the issues your future constituents care about are hiding in plain sight. Hadley Street is a four-lane divided highway that starts at Whittier Boulevard (our main thoroughfare) to the west and dead ends in a residential community, the Hadley Hills, to the east. Hadley separates the historic neighborhoods from the Uptown businesses and Whittier Central Park. The city originally intended for Hadley to connect to Colima Road, a large north-south artery. Bob, however, successfully opposed its expansion during his first stint on the council. Still, drivers frequently use Hadley to get to another busy artery, Painter Avenue, and some drag race down the steep slope starting at Elmquist Street (where Hadley ends). I wanted to be able to make it across the street with our massive double stroller without dodging cars. So, I drove to City Hall and complained. I requested a lighted crosswalk, and the city agreed to commission a traffic study. The city's department of public works opposed the crosswalk, arguing that there weren't enough pedestrians crossing the street (a Catch-22 given the dangers of walking across in the first place). The Parking and Transportation Commission hearing gave me a fantastic opportunity to bring people together to support a worthwhile project. With the help of my next-door neighbor, Candi Nash, a Republican originally from Friendly Hills, we mobilized the local community in support of the project.

We got at least a dozen people to come out and successfully lobby the commission. My status as a community advocate was cemented when a longtime resident came forward to say, "I've been wishing someone would help us put a crosswalk here for twenty years!" Getting involved taught me valuable lessons about what issues matter to residents (the closer to home, the more tangible the better), and how to cultivate and engage with volunteers (be clear about what they need to do and remind them multiple times). It also gave me a ready-made story for the campaign trail, which is indispensable when you're trying to build rapport with voters at the door.

After the crosswalk campaign succeeded, people started to ask if I would consider running. I fibbed. I didn't want anyone to know my intentions just yet lest some wolf in sheep's clothing should seek to undermine my fledgling candidacy. You might feel queasy about taking such a stealthy approach to what's effectively just community service. You might wonder whether anyone will believe you. In reality, few people actually follow-through and run for local office because of the expense and the time commitment. Denying you're running is, therefore, usually credible. Doing so helped me obtain a spot on the Social Services Commission when an opening came up about a year before the election. Had the council gotten wind of my candidacy, I almost certainly wouldn't have been appointed.

Perhaps you're considering being completely quiet and uninvolved until you're actually running, which is what two other candidates in my race, Vincent McLeod and Eric Leckey, did. You want to be a dark horse, though, not an invisible one. Going completely dark can lead to accusations that you're a puppet, placed in the race to stymie an insurgent candidate.

In short, the best approach when it comes to the buildup to a campaign is: get involved, get noticed, commit yourself only to issues that matter to both you and the community, and build momentum while also avoiding becoming a target for political opponents. Plausible deniability – being able to cast enough doubt about your intentions so that they can't be known to a certainty – is an essential aspect of being a come-from-behind candidate.

Admittedly, there's an "ick factor" at play when it comes to hiding your true intentions to advance your candidacy forward. That's why it's so crucial that you have solid reasons for running. Recently, an organization called "Run for Something" has been urging progressive candidates to run for local office. I prefer that you *run for a reason*. Running for a reason is what'll help you put aside your qualms about the occasionally disingenuous means and methods required for political success. Understanding what you're running for (the so-called long game) will you get past your initial qualms about the misdirection and sleight of hand that is sometimes necessary to ensure you aren't taken down early.

The sad fact that people have grown increasingly apathetic regarding local politics can actually work in your favor as a dark horse candidate. Making up the difference isn't at all out of the question for a no-name candidate since the absolute number of voters necessary to win an election (about a thousand in my case) can be fairly low.

With all of this said, when it comes to the pre-election stage (that is, the months and perhaps even years before you formally enter a race), what you do, how you do it, and who notices pales in comparison to precisely whom you do it with. I already mentioned my political consultant Danny and my college friend Daniel. We later added Gabriel Rodriguez, a former high school student of Daniel's and, like me, an avid Lakers fan, Candi Nash, my next door neighbor, and Caro Jauregui, a young Berkeley grad turned transportation advocate who later won a seat on the Whittier elementary school board.

By starting early and meeting regularly, usually over pizza and beers, we forged a bond that would be crucial to the race, Daniel keeping me grounded by mercilessly digging into me as only an old friend can do. As you'll learn, being a candidate can be a lonely business. Having people around you who feel comfortable telling you when your crap stinks is critical to keeping you humble and sane.

SUMMARY

- ∧ Build a portfolio of local activism based on your interests.
- ∧ You can't win if you don't take care of yourself and your loved ones.
- ∧ Scrutinize your motivations and get rid of them if they're not righteous.
- ∧ Ask yourself what story your membership in local groups tells.
- ∧ Community organizing is directly transferable to running for office.
- ∧ You'll find opportunities to make a difference all around you if you look closely.
- ∧ It's okay to deny you're running until the time is right.
- ∧ Surround yourself with good people.

PART III

CAMPAIGNING

"Politicians are not born; they are excreted."

– **CICERO**

CHAPTER 8

YOU NEED PROFESSIONAL HELP

There's limited literature out there about running a local campaign for elected office. Much of it focuses on the Xs and Os of getting on the ballot. These books want to make you into a campaign manager or political consultant when what you should be focusing on is being a candidate. Your time should ideally be directed at what will win you the race: winning hearts and minds. Delegate the rest.

Remember, if done right, running for local elected office should a life-altering experience. Don't be cheap or cut corners. Hire a professional to help you. As a first-time candidate, you're inherently at a disadvantage in that you're unfamiliar with the nuances of running for office, and no book alone will catch you up quickly enough. A competent political consultant will get you up to speed and alert you to your blind spots.

Before I get into how to choose a political consultant and what to look for in one, let me explain what a political consultant does. First, a political consultant isn't a campaign manager. A campaign manager is a part-time or even full-time employee or volunteer who manages your campaign's day-to-day aspects.[21] A political consultant, on the other hand, focuses on the bigger picture, the so-called forest for the trees, allowing you to avoid getting sidetracked by day-to-day campaign distractions.According to The Campaign Workshop, a political consulting firm:

A political consultant has a treasure trove of experience, having worked on campaigns across the country in different capacities for a long time. A [consultant] knows the ins and outs of campaigns and will work with you to craft a strategy for your race. A consultant can be an incredibly invaluable resource [particularly] if your campaign manager doesn't have a ton of experience. While your [consultant] won't perform day-to-day tasks like call time and door-knocking (nor should they), they will leverage their expertise to help you build a winning campaign plan, solve problems, and spend your budget efficiently and effectively.

Some, including The Campaign Workshop, argue that a campaign manager is more essential than a political consultant. I disagree. A campaign manager completes the mundane or repetitive tasks you likely would prefer not to do but could do if necessary. A good campaign manager will save you time, but a good political consultant will save your campaign. It's the difference between doing the wrong thing right and the right thing wrong. You hire a political consultant because a failed strategy executed flawlessly, by definition, cannot succeed, whereas a winning strategy can work despite potential mistakes and growing pains.

Assessing Your Options

Depending on where you live, you might have access to several political consultants, or you might have none. Even in places like Southern California, where there are thousands of consultants, the pickings can be slim for the local candidate. You can start your search online, but, in all likelihood, you'll find a consultant by mining your network. Because the total amounts raised in local races aren't considerable, you may be relegated to choosing either an inexperienced wannabe making his or her bones on your race or an old hat who doesn't have much time for you. Timing can also play a factor in the availability of consultants. I was lucky in this sense in that Whittier's election was off-cycle in April at the time (most other local elections are held during the November general election or the primary), meaning that my consultant could afford to give me extra attention since I was his only April race. For instance, he took the time to help set up my first day of canvassing and held a debate prep session with my team and me.

Avoid the inexperienced or first-time consultant altogether if you can. As a newbie candidate, having an inexperienced consultant is like the blind leading the blind. Finding an experienced consultant who will work with you can be challenging, though. It's understandable why an experienced consultant would give you the short shrift. Pay in the four figures simply can't justify spending lavish amounts of time on your race. To represent you, the experienced consultant may need to take on additional clients to balance things out. That means when it gets close to election time, you're going to be triaged accordingly. To get a good consultant to commit resources to you, you'll have to go out there and network and make a good case for yourself as I did with Danny. If you can show an experienced consultant that you have promise and take your race seriously, they'll consider committing to you as a long-term business investment (since consultants make money through re-elections and when they do communications work for school districts and municipal governments).

Take the time to get to know your consultant personally before pulling the trigger. When Danny and I discussed his experience at Navy Officer Candidates School in Newport, Rhode Island, where I was stationed for Naval Justice School, I became hopeful. We would understand each other like only two people who've experienced the utter frustration of trying to make a perfect bed in ten seconds at five in the morning while being screamed at before rushing out the door for ammo can thrusts can.

Getting the Most Out of Your Consultant

Once you do hire a consultamt, it helps to treat them like a partner and not a punching bag. Running for office gets incredibly stressful, especially when the unexpected happens. Don't be a candidate prima donna. Treat your consultant with patience, respect, and understanding. Trust me, it pays off. Also, political consultants are a bit of a mafia, so mistreating one can cause you difficulties down the road. At the same time, you need to have the courage and confidence to tell your consultant when you're dissatisfied. On one such occasion, I could tell something was wrong because Danny was quite pessimistic during a strategy meeting with our campaign team. In retrospect, he might've been getting some blowback for taking me on as a client (since I was running against an established politician and they tend to have powerful friends). I pulled him aside afterward and let him know how much I valued him but that I needed more than just his time.

"I need you to *believe*, Danny. We're going to win this thing, but only if you have faith. And the others need to see it from you, or we're not gonna make it." To be a politician is to be a leader (at least it's supposed to be). Don't wait until after your election to act like one. Make your consultant feel like part of a team, a cause. Although consultants can sometimes come across as jaded, they're idealists at heart. They're usually people who started their careers as young, bright-eyed campaign volunteers. To his credit, Danny had the maturity and humility to accept my constructive criticism and jump in with both feet.

Delegate Work, Not Responsibility

Make sure to avoid relying too much on your consultant. While it's true that you'll want to delegate a significant amount of your activities, particularly the closer you get to the election, you've got to make sure you're the one running your campaign. While delegating the mundane, esoteric, or repetitive is smart (and ideally, you'll have a campaign manager for that), hoping someone other than you will care as much as you do about the critical components of your campaign is foolhardy. Think of your consultant as a guide who will take you from campaign novice to veteran. Seek to understand why certain actions are being taken on your behalf and insist on giving consent for important decisions like what final language goes on your mailers. In other words, trust but verify.

I met someone running for political office in Los Angeles around the same time as me at his kickoff fundraiser. He had both the look and the sound down, speaking Bernie with an Obama delivery, except he made a fatal mistake. Despite being a promising candidate, he lost handily, forced to run a write-in campaign, which is next to impossible win, because he lacked enough signatures to get on the ballot. Most jurisdictions require you to obtain a certain number of signatures on a petition to qualify. In Whittier, it's twenty, although you can submit as many as 30 to be safe. They give you a short window, a week or so, to submit them and get them verified. This *de minimus* requirement is presumably intended to make the bar to entry just high enough to avoid dozens, or even hundreds, of gadflies on the ballot.

I made sure to get all 30 signatures. I submitted them several days early just in case some were unreadable or the signer wasn't a registered voter. This candidate did not, relying on his consultant to handle this for him. What had started as a promising candidacy ended up as an embarrassing loss for him. Don't let this happen to you. Trust but verify. A consultant is there for consultation, not to do your job for you.

Paying for Consulting

As far as how much hiring a consultant can cost, this varies widely, of course. We agreed on $10,000 for my 2018 race. That might sound like a lot, but, as the saying goes, you get what you pay for. You don't want to skimp out on the person who will be your key advisor, your guide, during this process. The most expensive consultant, however, isn't necessarily going to be the best one for you. Like any job, this is all about fit. Move on if you don't feel comfortable asking your prospective consultant questions, even silly ones. Pass if the consultant has a conflict of interest. The last thing you want is to get dragged unwittingly into somebody else's war.

What a political consultant does also varies. Some handle mail design and distribution only. Others handle a wider range of activities, including social media, web design, video, and print advertising. Take the time to write out a contract with your consultant that details, line-by-line, what services they will provide and what the consultant expects from you. After all, this is a two-way street.

The best consultants for local races will also be well-versed in the local issues and personalities, whether because they live in the area and participate in local politics or because they used to work for a local elected official. Whatever the case, you want someone who can talk strategy and not just messaging. Your messaging plan can't be developed in a vacuum. It has to consider your strengths and weaknesses and that of your opponents, as well as the political climate and local current events and trends. Danny had been the field representative for state assemblyman Ian Calderon, so he knew all the key players in Whittier.

Make sure to shop around, speaking to at least two or three consultants before landing on one and, if possible, ask for a discount for paying in one lump sum. Like I said, though, don't balk at the financial commitment. Once you have a good consultant, you're in better shape than some Tom, Dick, and Harry armed with nothing more than a guidebook and a prayer.

SUMMARY

^ Don't be cheap. Hire a professional.

^ A political consultant can be more valuable than a campaign manager, especially if you're new to politics and willing to put in work.

^ Hire a consultant with experience.

^ Get to know your consultant before you hire them.

^ Treat your consultant as a partner and learn from them.

^ Services provided by consultants vary. Draft up a contract.

^ You get what you pay for.

CHAPTER 9

THE ART OF BUDGETING

You're probably wondering, "How much do I need to spend on my race?" How much you're going to need will largely depend on the size of your constituency. I spent about $50,000 in a district of 20,000 people. However, your amount may vary depending on the timing of the election – whether it's a primary, general, or special election, the ratio of low to high propensity voters, and the amount of money your opponent is likely to spend. You'll need to perform some careful budgeting to figure out exactly how much you're going to need.

Cash (Flow) is King

In business school, they describe cash flow as the money transferred in and out of a given business. Cash flow, both inflows and outflows, is considered a critical aspect of a particular business's desirability. You're taught that it's not just the *quantity* but also the *quality* of your cash flow, meaning the total amount of money going in and out *and its timing*. You can have a lucrative business that goes belly up because the money wasn't there when you needed it to be.

You can also get in trouble for not spending money in a timely way. For instance, I recently reviewed the final financial disclosures for my race, the ones that extend from the week before the election to several months afterward. Irella Perez failed to spend

$4,187.73, or roughly a tenth of her earnings. She ran out of time before she ran out of money. She likely spent more time thinking about how to come up with money than how to spend it all.

Other candidates spend all their money, but they spend it on items unlikely to increase their chances of winning. They give themselves the sense that they're going all out by paying for trinkets, extra consultants, or unneeded office space. They pay for additional mailers after the principle of diminishing returns dictates those mailers will be ineffectual.

Pro Forma Like a Pro

The antidote to such wastefulness is the pro forma budget. Pro forma just means working draft. In January of 2018, Danny and I went through every item that we expected to spend on during the election, line by line. At this stage, I had already raised about $15,000 and loaned myself another $10,000. With that in mind, we built a budget of $34,095 to work from. Some of the expenses were obvious: $12,000 for mailers, $2,000 for lawn signs, and $1,500 for a walking piece, the handout you give voters at the door while canvassing. Other expenses only a political consultant like Danny would know to include, such as the cost of field supplies for volunteers, a small budget for targeting visitors to the website with follow-up ads, and a small allotment for events (coffee klatches, meet-and-greets, and the like). Finally, there were miscellaneous expenses like the $495 filing fee, the cost of political data, and a fee for canvassing software. Add what monies you have on hand, and you more or less have what they refer to in business parlance as a balance sheet.

Don't stop there, though. Next is perhaps the most critical aspect of the campaign budget. Make sure to break down expenses by month (what's known as a cash flow statement) so that you set the benchmarks necessary to make your budget work for you.

Be Ready to Make Strategic Decisions

Creating a budget early not only permits you to set up (and step up) your fundraising efforts; it also helps you to develop a strategy by forcing you to decide what matters and what doesn't. This puts you and your political consultant on the same page and ensures you're working within your financial constraints. Be ready to make hard decisions at the budget setting stage. Avoid the urge to kick the can, leaving important strategic choices for later. You can always adjust course down the road.

Don't just take the kitchen sink approach either. Few, if any, candidates are good at all aspects of campaigning. Some are good at fundraising, while others are excellent debaters or speechmakers. Still others are great at what's known as retail politics, a style of political campaigning in which the candidate attends local events to target voters on a small-scale or individual basis. (Irella was great at such schmoozing). Almost no one can put together a stellar campaign in every single aspect of being a candidate. You likely have a particular knack for one or more features of "campaignery." For you, it might be public speaking and glad-handing. For someone else (like Bob), it might be name recognition and relationship building.

For me, the act of budgeting led to two of the most significant strategic decisions in my race. The first was to set a sizeable digital budget of $6,000, about a sixth of our budget, most of that dedicated to Facebook ads. I knew I could work Facebook. The platform came out when I was a freshman in college at Loyola Marymount, and I had used it through college, law school, and beyond. I was confident I could create compelling content, which paid ads would give additional legs.

I also decided to set aside some money, $1,500, for paid canvassers, that is, people who knock on doors and ask for votes on your behalf for money. This was a somewhat unusual move for a campaign of our size (paid canvassing is usually reserved for larger races). I'm someone who cultivates close, long-term friendships. I foresaw rightly that my friends might drop what they were doing and dedicate themselves to my campaign with a little financial support. These decisions, made at the budgeting stage, proved to be difference makers on election night.

Diversify Your Expenditures

Diversification is yet another basic business principle, which applies to a campaign. Don't become over-reliant on any one particular means of campaigning. Don't fall in love with mail, for instance, to the detriment of other vital messaging techniques. While mailers are one of the most persuasive, and expensive, form of paid political advertising, they don't create a personal, human connection.

At the same time, don't rely exclusively on canvassing. Upstart candidates tend to overestimate their ability to knock on more doors than their opponents. They become enamored with stories of candidates who walked endlessly in pursuit of their goal. The problem with this approach is that there are only ten weeks or so leading up to an election during which residents care to open their doors to you in a receptive matter. Start too early and you run the risk of being off-putting, invading people's hard-earned privacy. The human body, moreover, has its limits. I waged a herculean effort, personally hitting around 5,000 doors. Even then, I only spoke to about 1,200 voters since not every voter was home or answered the door.

Ensure your various forms of communication – online ads, social media, mail, and person-to-person – complement each other and that you have a clear, consistent message. That means your budget and your communications strategy should match up. (You shouldn't have more money in your budget set aside for phone banking than mailers, for instance, if your focus will be on sending mailers). Treat your campaign like a *popularity business* and not a *popularity contest*. It pays off

There are several dividends to this type of budgeting, including the confidence to purchase printed materials in bulk, providing you with the "economies of scale" large purchases offer. Taking the spaghetti approach – throwing stuff against the wall and hoping that it sticks – is a recipe for wastefulness. Such an ad hoc, reactive approach to your spending will invariably result in wasteful, trial-and-error purchases that are neither successful nor respectful of those who have donated their hard-earned income to your venture.

Understand How Your Opponents Fundraise

You should also analyze your competitors' fundraising and spending habits. It's easy to get this information from your registrar or clerk. Just ask. By doing so, I learned, for instance, that Bob liked to wait until quite late in the election cycle to start his fundraising efforts. I used this knowledge to develop a stealth fundraising strategy, raising funds primarily from outside Whittier at the outset and lulling Bob into a state of complacency, which he had difficulty recovering from.

Conclusion

I hope I'm not making it seem like you need a business degree to run a campaign. You can be a total right-brained person and run a killer campaign. You can run circles around opponents even if you don't know your way around a spreadsheet. You don't even need to know long division. What you do need is a willingness to ask the right questions and to think ahead. Numbers can be intimidating, especially when you have to ask others to give you the money you need. This can make almost any person want to bury their heads in the sand and put off the budget until later. But you can't. Budgeting is ultimately less about money than it is about making decisions. And the person who makes better decisions, and arrives at them quicker, usually wins the race.

SUMMARY

- ^ When you raise money matters as much as how much.
- ^ Budgeting is about helping you reach strategic decisions.
- ^ Accentuate your strengths within your budget.
- ^ Don't waste your hard-earned money on gimmicks.
- ^ Analyze the past spending habits of your opponents.

RESOURCES

For a sample budget, an explanation of accounting concepts and terms, and instructions on how to discover your opponents' past expenses, go to authorhenrybouchot.com.

CHAPTER 10

SHOW ME THE MONEY

I mentioned that few, if any, candidates are good at all facets of campaigning. Most, however, are bad at fundraising. Asking for money is hard. It's time-consuming and filled with rejection, sort of like dating.

I started by calling people in my phone alphabetically. The first person to answer was Bobby, a former co-worker. "Hey, Bobby, what's been up, man?" We caught up on family and work developments, old Marine Corps memories, and the like. Then, the awkward transition: "Listen, did I mention that I'm running for office?" Nothing makes you feel sleazier than calling someone you haven't spoken to in months and hitting them up for money.

While it's tempting to leave the painful ask until the end, nothing can be more off-putting. Even if it's been years, be upfront and start the call by saying something like, "I know we haven't spoken for a while, and I want to know what you've been up to, but I need to be upfront and let you know I'm calling to ask for money for an important cause." You might get turned down this way, but at least you won't ruin a friendship. Fortunately for me, Bobby is a magnanimous, easy going-guy.

Track Your Efforts

While my initial fundraising tactics were rough, I did get better over time. I became more confident and direct about what I was calling for. Importantly, I kept a Microsoft Excel tracker from the start, indicating whom I had reached out to and when, the method of contact (whether Facebook Messenger, email, text, call, or in-person), and whether they had promised to donate. This provided me with several advantages down the road. For one, it allowed me to follow up with delinquent donors (by text and, if necessary, with a follow-up call) in a systematic way. Over time, I refined my list, categorizing potential donors using various color schemes based on the likelihood of donating (truth is some people will only donate if your campaign looks like a winner). Using this method, I was always speaking with the person most likely to contribute to me at any given time. The tracker came in particularly handy during the later stages of the campaign when I had exhausted my network and began to double back to ask the earliest donors for additional donations since I knew whom to start with first.

Mine Your Contacts

List-making also helped me to tap into groups to which I belonged. I sent emails to my MBA cohort at Mount Saint Mary's University and my colleagues at the Southern California Leadership Network's Leadership L.A. program. Consider reaching out to any civic-minded groups you're a member of as they're likely to be invested in your career success.

Using a tracker forced me to think carefully about who in my network I could contact. I poured over my Facebook friends and phone contacts. I categorized people by the stage in life when we had met, including family, college, law school, business school, and so on. While being a relative newcomer to Whittier had plenty of disadvantages, it had one significant advantage in that I could raise a substantial amount of money from people outside the city, leaving my competitors with no clue of the strength of my campaign until it was too late.

Fundraise Strategically

Given that the first campaign finance deadline (the date when your financial disclosures statements are due) for the period leading up to December 31, 2017 wasn't until January 31, 2018, my opponents wouldn't know how much I'd raised until just weeks before the election. Having reviewed his past fundraising disclosures, I suspected Bob might not start fundraising until late. I learned from my research that he typically put off fundraising until January or February and then raised just enough money to ward off his competitors. By fundraising primarily from non-local donors, I hoped to catch Bob off-guard. My strategy worked. By the time of the first fundraising deadline, Bob was already well behind. Your strategy might look different than mine. If you have access to cash, you might loan yourself a large sum right off the bat to give the perception that you're committed to doing whatever it takes to win. Or you might show how broad your grassroots support is by cultivating many small donations. Whatever your choice, let your strategy be your guide.

Limit Fundraising Events

Most campaigns take a much different approach from mine. They don't bother to hide their fundraising activity and instead start with a big campaign kickoff fundraiser. While such a fundraiser is a fun way to get a campaign going, I would caution you against hosting multiple fundraising events. Fundraisers are inefficient because they take an inordinate amount of time to organize if done right, robbing you of time better spent on other campaign activities.

I learned this the hard way when I put weeks of effort into hosting a fundraiser for my college buddies only to net around $250 for my troubles. Part of the problem was they weren't experienced in giving to political causes. Part of it was I failed to set clear expectations for them. Regardless, you'll find that even among people who understand political giving, the upfront costs and time investment involved in planning a fundraiser (everything from deciding on when and where to host the event to the types of napkins, hors d'oeuvres, and color of the balloons) can quickly make a fundraiser a money loser.

Admittedly, event planning isn't my strength. Some people just have a knack, a love even, for organizing events. My wife, Christina, for example, organized our wedding in five weeks (long story). And it came off wonderfully. If you're one of these people, well, great for you. Remember, though, that your end goal is not to host the best fundraiser but to have the best campaign.

Move Your Fundraising Online

Unlike in-person fundraising events, online fundraisers can be a highly efficient way to raise money as supporters can donate from the comfort of their homes. After discovering the limitations of in-person fundraising soirées, I turned to Facebook to raise money, creating an event page, a monetary goal, and a deadline of a week or so. I set the end of the fundraiser event to coincide with a reporting deadline. I then created content each day on why I was running as well as the key issues and latest developments. This worked better than I expected, with me raising thousands of dollars at a time. What made it effective, I suspect, is that people like being acknowledged publicly for their donations. By giving people online props for their contributions, my Facebook fundraisers became group endeavors.

There are other platforms for fundraising. Ask your political consultant for recommendations. Your consultant might even recommend that you hire a professional fundraiser. A fundraising consultant will help you organize yourself in a systematic way. They charge either a percentage of your earnings or a fixed amount. If you feel you need someone to hold you accountable to your fundraising goals, then knock yourself out.

Reaching Out

Unfortunately, you can't rely exclusively on online fundraising. Phone calls are the bread and butter of effective fundraising. (No need to meet people in person, by the way, unless they're going to give a sizable donation. It's just too time-consuming, especially in L.A. traffic). Always call potential donors to make the first ask. Don't start by texting. It's too impersonal. They say a fool and his money are soon parted. Well, only a fool expects others to part with their cash without asking first. Pick up the phone and dial. If they don't answer, then (and only then) send a text.

Texting, however, can be helpful as a follow-up tool once you have made your initial round of calls, particularly as you get close to a fundraising deadline when you're pressed for time. However, you must avoid sending group text messages at all costs. It's simply too easy to ignore a group text asking for money: "Hi friends!

I'm running for office and need your help," screams, "I didn't bother to reach out to you directly because you're not important to me!" Take the time to text each person individually. Include an ask such as, "Can I still count on you?" Make it so that they have to respond to you, even if it's a no. It's easier, psychologically, to ignore a group text without a specific ask than a targeted message asking someone to follow through on a commitment.

Knowing when to phone people can also be a challenge. Calling during the weekend feels like an intrusion. Calling during work seems like an excellent way to alienate a person, which means the best hours are limited to after work. The problem is that with the decline of the typical nine-to-five work schedule, "after work" has little definite meaning any more. I've heard the mornings are best since people aren't stressed out yet, but I'm not sure. I was pretty stressed out by 9 when my kids were in diapers. Calling and asking for money is like ripping off a Band-Aid. Just get it over with as soon as possible.

What to Say

There are no magic words. What matters is that you sincerely convey the importance and the urgency of your cause. Explain why your city will be better off, and the world for that matter (if only in a small way), with you as an elected official. The people you're going to be targeting with this message already know you and will thus be inclined to help you. However, you still have to make them feel that they're doing good, not just giving money to an egotistical politician looking to promote his or her self-interest. (Make sure, by the way, to inform donors that political donations aren't tax-deductible). Don't get discouraged if you don't rack up enormous contributions early on. Some people hold on to their cash until you've shown you're committed and viable. That's where your tracker comes in handy as you circle back to potential donors later on in the campaign.

How Much to Request

How much you ask for is another tricky question. Conventional wisdom says to ask for three times the amount you think the donor would give. There's some truth to this. On the other hand, I asked a college friend who is a lawyer for $250, hoping for at least $100. He said yes but ended up giving me $25. If you're on the younger side, many of your contacts may have limited giving power. Regardless of how much you request, your donors will provide what their hearts and wallets permit (one of my high school friends touchingly gave me $50 even though he and his fiancée were sleeping on a couch). One of Christina's friends gave $500 when I'd expected $50. While you should have a dollar figure in mind when you ask for money, the point is to get something. You want to develop a giving relationship. Even if they give just a nominal amount to start, they'll be more inclined to give additional donations as the race progresses. Some people are willing to make small monthly donations. If you can, enroll these people into automatic payments as this helps you maintain steady cash flow.

Processing Donations

You can obtain donations through cash, check, or via online payment. I prefer the latter. It's less labor-intensive, makes tracking donations more manageable, and simplifies the process of compiling campaign finance disclosure paperwork later on. For me, reaching out to people across the country, and throughout Southern California, made a focus on online giving necessary. Admittedly, using online payment processing may cost you a small fee tacked onto each donation. Still, I would argue it's worth the cost.

Budget for a professional campaign treasurer if you want to make your life easy. They'll ensure you avoid disclosure improprieties and help you stay focused on earning votes instead of mashing a calculator. Treasurers aren't cheap, but they're a worthwhile luxury, especially as the campaign nears its close.

Another advantage of using online payment processing is the ability to suggest higher donation amounts without the awkwardness. People can be highly suggestible. Their donation amount will change depending on the options. Use a "good, better, best" model such as $100, $150, $250, and people will invariably pick the middle option. Play around with the payment amounts to inch your averages up over time. Ultimately, my average donation was about $90. I probably could have increased it had I started with a higher minimum amount.

Please and Thank You

Above all else, make sure to personally thank your donors. If at all possible, take the time to print out a thank you letter on campaign letterhead signed in your hand. It signals to donors that you're running a professional campaign and that you genuinely appreciate their contribution. If you don't have the time, either because of a busy schedule or the campaign is in full swing, send a text or put in a call at the very least. Without this personal touch, don't expect to get a second (or even third) donation. For me, subsequent contributions accounted for about a third of my total revenue.

Ultimately, what you're asking when you request a donation is for people to buy into you. You want to make sure they have a satisfying customer experience. That means being polite and personal when you call and expressing thanks in a sincere, meaningful way.

Leverage an Email Newsletter for Donations

The beauty of using an online donation system is that it'll ask donors to enter an email address (whereas a check obviously doesn't have this feature). You can then have a member of your team use an email marketing platform, to send out updates on how the campaign is going. This helps your donors feel like they're a part of your campaign, whether or not they're active participants. My next-door neighbor Candi, who previously worked in marketing, volunteered to take my Facebook posts and other content and distill them into a newsletter using Mailchimp, and it worked incredibly well. One neighbor Candi introduced to me so appreciated the newsletters that she, no kidding, donated $1,000 each time we sent one. Turning the map around and thinking of fundraising as something the donor experiences, rather than as painful drudgery for you, can make a dramatic difference.

Capitalize on Success

Through fundraising, I was able to establish myself as a legitimate candidate. The voters found out that I wasn't just some fly-by-night once they read the local news coverage of our campaign finance filings.[22] Thanks to my fundraising prowess, I was able to shock the establishment candidates despite not having the same degree of institutional support. People like to place money on a winner. Once word got out that I had the means to put together a competitive campaign, local donors began seeking me out. I was elated. My campaign was finally started to feel a tailwind. By starting early and working hard, I took the lead and never looked back, my early success turning into a self-fulfilling, self-perpetuating prophecy.

Money Isn't Everything (or The Only Thing)

Be careful not to rely too heavily on fundraising as your bid for success. It's not the answer to everything. Raise too much money, or rely just on one source of funds, and your opponents can shape a narrative that will undermine you. If you have deep pockets and decide to completely self-fund, you'll be described as a rich snob. If you raise funds from one source of funding to the exclusion of others, they will label you as a puppet.

This happened to Lizette Escobedo, a 2018 candidate for Whittier's Council District 4, who received significant funding from her powerful service employees' union. Whatever the merits of unionized labor, her opponent was able to successfully characterize her as an outsider.[23] There's an old joke that goes, "There are two things that are important in politics. The first is money, and I can't remember what the second one is." What I would say is there are two important things when running for office. The first is money. The second is handling money wisely. Had Lizette spread her union donations over a more extended period, she might have prevented her opponents from maligning her.

While some candidates believe, wrongly, that money fixes all problems, others naively equate all forms of money with improper influence and refuse to raise funds from any donors. I was, and am, proud of my 300-plus donations because they came exclusively from individual donors. It showed that I had grassroots support. Not raising money, conversely, makes you seem like you're not taking the race seriously. Suck it up and do the hard work of getting the cash you need to win.

SUMMARY

- ^ Cut to the chase with donors.
- ^ Follow up regularly and systematically with donors.
- ^ Always start by calling. Leave text for follow-up.
- ^ There are no magic words. Just be sincere.
- ^ Every dollar counts, even small donations matter.
- ^ Hire a treasurer to be safe. Mind your disclosure deadlines.
- ^ Thank your donors.
- ^ Email lists are great for donation requests.
- ^ Money without strategy is wasted.
- ^ In-person fundraisers have a dubious return on investment.

RESOURCES

For a list of online fundraising platforms and processors, an example thank-you letter, and a sample tracker, check out authorhenrybouchot.com.

CHAPTER 11

A BRAND NEW YOU

So, you have some money, an idea of how you're going to use it, a small team around you to provide some help – what now? Do you jump right in and start knocking on your neighbors' doors at random? Not quite. Before you can get your campaign going, you'll first need to decide on your brand. Your brand is how people perceive you. You must think carefully about how you want to be perceived as a politician to ensure those perceptions are positive and in line with your strategy and who you are. You might not be selling a product for money, but when you ask people for their votes, you're not asking for a favor. You're selling them yourself, your identity, and your vision for the community.

Your Platform

Perhaps more than any other aspect of your campaign, your policy goals, or "platform," distinguishes you from other candidates. It's what discerning voters look to first when making their choice about who to support. A carefully developed platform infuses your campaign with meaning.

Your bio can inform your platform but don't confuse the two. Local voters want elected officials who will improve their quality of life as much as they want someone with whom they can relate. So, your family came to America with no money on a canoe and you paid your way through Harvard by shining shoes? Good for you, but what's that mean to the average voter? You'd be the first biracial, transgender, atheist on the city council? That's great, but what are you going to do to reduce homelessness and crime? How are you going to balance the budget amidst rising pension costs? What is your plan to address worsening traffic? You must explain how your background and experience will allow you to solve your community's pressing problems. Don't expect the voters to make the connection on their own, as you may not like the conclusions they draw.

While your platform should be inclusive, don't try to please everyone. In politics as in life, trying to make everyone happy is a surefire way of making yourself miserable. It can also blow up in your face if, for example, you're caught on camera making contradictory promises. Your platform will invariably alienate some and draw in others. That's because a platform is a list of what you consider the most significant obstacles facing your community and your framework for addressing them. People will inevitably disagree with you about what the most significant challenges are and the best way to address them. That's okay. You don't need 100% of the votes to win.

Your platform is both art and science. The science part comes from predicting which demographic groups will turn out for a given election. The art comes in framing the issues in a way that galvanizes these voters. And by "issues," I mean local matters. Leave purely federal concerns like immigration reform, entitlements, or foreign policy to those running for Congress. Don't focus on education either (unless you're running for school board, of course). To identify critical local issues, you'll need to get out into the community and experience life as your future constituents do. If something frustrates you, it likely also frustrates your neighbors. And they'll probably talk about it on NextDoor, at the Senior Center, at City Hall during public comment, in various community Facebook groups, and in the newspaper.

What will set your platform apart from others is your creativity in formulating answers to your municipality's problems. Key issues will likely jump out at you reasonably quickly. In my area of Whittier, it was crime, homelessness, housing development, traffic, and the beautification of Uptown. It didn't take a genius to figure that out. Coming up with creative, practical solutions was the hard part. Showing that you have thoughtful ways of solving problems demonstrates why you're the best fit for the job.

Knowing what people want most before drafting your platform is critical. However, I don't want you to get the impression that you should simply parrot back what people are complaining about. Even though Whittier's hottest issues were homelessness, public safety, and development, I went with the platform, "Safety, Transparency, and Prosperity." Arguably, I left out the most crucial issue: housing construction. Irella made opposing home building her case, even though California was, and is, facing a housing shortage. She spoke about keeping the "charm" that makes up Whittier, "no to high rises," and so forth. While her position was probably music to many voters' ears, Irella came across as insincere to me.

Call me an idealist, but I simply can't fight for something I don't believe in. Instead of opposing residential development, I homed in on a deeper issue, public trust. I deduced that voter dissatisfaction had less to do with opposition to development than with feelings of fear and mistrust. I knew people were upset about several issues, including the potential for new oil drilling in the hills. They were concerned with the council's costly opposition to districting, with a proposed budget motel on a boulevard saturated with them,[24] and with the habitat's closure to hikers except during working hours and on weekends.[25] Residents felt their impact on local government affairs was limited. By focusing on transparency and accountability, I could provide voters with a calming sense of agency and empowerment.

The bottom line is you will need to find ways to incorporate primal feelings, not merely staid issues, into your platform. Without tapping into public sentiment, the chances of getting people to come out and unseat an incumbent are low. Your ability to enthusiastically and credibly embrace your issues is, moreover, immensely helpful in bringing skeptical voters to your side.

Safety is a perennial concern for local governments. It was a particularly important issue here with a recent spike in property crime. Homelessness was too. I could have pandered to the not-in-my-back-yard crowd by offering to leaf-blow homeless people or by vowing to enact draconian criminalization policies. That, however, would not have been in keeping with my beliefs. Rather than fall into the traditional public safety trap and behave in an inauthentic "tough on crime" way, I placed my own spin on the subject. I focused on something less polarizing yet no less critical: police response times. Through a public record request, I discovered that police response times had increased steadily due in part to a rise in people calling to report homeless people on the streets.

Safety was a particularly charged issue in Whittier at the time. On President's Day 2017, a fleeing felon, Michael Mejia, gunned down a Whittier Police Officer named Keith Boyer.

Boyer had come to Medina's aid after he crashed his vehicle.[26] Later, Mayor Joe Vinatieri would join with Assemblyman Ian Calderon to roll back certain criminal justice reforms.[27] Governor Jerry Brown, however, vetoed the bill.

Many blamed the increased crime on recent criminal justice reform measures. No one, however, was addressing the slower response times and the increased strain homelessness-related 911 calls were having. I sent out a mailer with an infographic highlighting this concern, undermining Bob's case that he was a steady hand when it came to safety. Irella, meanwhile, put out statistics about the amount of crime in Whittier *per mile*, which were immediately discounted by informed readers since crime per capita is the more accurate metric.

The third plank of my platform was "prosperity." Even though we had come a long way since the Great Recession, it still felt like the city was stuck in small-town ways of doing business. My goal in seeking election was to connect Whittier's diverse assets – historical, recreational, culinary, and architectural – in a cohesive way.[28] That would mean greater investment in public transportation and a renewed focus on our Uptown area. It would mean focusing away from big box stores and fast-food chains, positioning the city as a regional destination.

Offering to deliver prosperity might've been overpromising on my part, but this is better than the alternative of focusing exclusively on small picture ideas that don't resonate with voters. For instance, the wine salesman I ran against, Eric Leckey, promised to create a citizens' commission to explore Whittier's lack of cable television options. Aside from the impracticality of a local government wading into federal telecom concerns, this was a minor issue for voters at best. Sure, paying high prices for NFL Game Pass and dealing with bad customer service is annoying. However, voters want their local politicians to focus on bedrock issues, not red herrings.

A creative platform will go a long distance toward differentiating you. When you participate in debates, having a fresh perspective will set you apart. I'm assuming your ideas aren't off the wall like the Whittier mayoral candidate who promised to hire hundreds of police officers to protect against the "thousands" of pedophiles he claimed resided in the city. Focus on the most important questions to your neighbors and then learn their intricacies. In other words, know what you're talking about. Speak with your neighbors and learn their concerns. Be able to explain how these problems came about and what it takes to solve them.

In the months leading up to announcing my campaign, I toured the local Boys & Girls Club. I went to an exhibit at the Whittier Museum commemorating the 30th Anniversary of the Whittier Narrows Earthquake. I attended a meet-and-greet with the legislative staff for our various state and federal elected officials. I even participated in a general plan input meeting at our historic train depot. I sat in on council meetings involving hot topics like a motel moratorium, the closure of the hiking trails, and the council's decision to oppose Measure M, a regional transportation tax hike. I even went on a ride-along with Whittier police. By the time I sat down to choose my platform, I knew which issues would move the needle with voters and which would not.

It's not enough to simply pick the issues people are currently upset about. Online, people scream about anything and everything. Disneyland increasing its prices sadly, receives more outrage than a boat of refugees capsizing off the Mediterranean. Voting, however, is a much more complicated endeavor than clicking the like button on Facebook. Plus, voters move on from issues quickly. That's where Irella made a mistake in trying to galvanize voters against development. By the time of the election, the issue didn't have the same currency. Instead, anticipate what issues will matter come election time. Keep in mind that incumbents will commonly refrain from taking up controversial items in the months or weeks leading up to the election. In some cases, incumbents bolster their campaigns with last-minute maneuvers. For instance, Bob secured a settlement between the Whittier Conservancy and Brookfield Residential to begin construction on the long-stalled Nelles former correctional facility development just weeks before election day.[29]

Deep down, voters want you to lead, not follow. Rosalynn Carter said, "A leader takes people where they want to go. A great leader takes people where they don't necessarily want to go but ought to be." Have guts. Don't follow. If categorically opposing development is a bad idea for your community, explain why and give people a more nuanced alternative they can embrace. If the prevailing narrative for why calls for service have spiked is that criminals are overrunning your community, but the reality is that crime remains low by historical standards, explain why an information campaign is merited instead of a crackdown. If you want to lead your city, don't wait until you're elected.

Your Logo

In an ideal world, a campaign would simply be a battle of the platforms. Voters would be well-versed in the underlying policy concerns at stake and take the time to thoroughly research the candidates. Of course, we don't live in a perfect world. Voters lead busy lives and aren't as knowledgeable about local politics as you might hope. That's why visual cues become so critical to a race. If you can find a way to use optical means to convey your campaign's essence simply and boldly, you stand a much better chance of convincing voters to side with you.

First up are your color scheme and your logo. Give some genuine thought to this. Many candidates default to a patriotic red, white, and blue color scheme. The problem is this doesn't help you stand out from the competition. What are you trying to convey, that you're American, that you love America? Well, duh. Some nonconformists go to the opposite extreme and pick colors that are loud and attention-grabbing. Bob had historically used "Henderson Orange" for his logo and lawn signs. While getting attention is a good thing, you want to make sure that attention is positive and not merely obnoxious. The longer Bob's bright orange lawn signs were out, the more annoying they became.

I went with blue-purple lettering. I listed "Henry" above "Bouchot" with my last name in large, bold letters. Below a pumpkin-colored orange line was "for Whittier City Council." I left the name of the district out because it would add wordiness to the logo, and only voters in the district would be able to vote for me anyway.

When I was working with the designer, I had the idea of making the logo resemble a bungalow. I expected housing and homelessness would be major campaign issues, plus I lived in a historic district with a number of Craftsman homes. Danny cautioned against it as voters might miss the point or confuse the logo for a housing nonprofit. Those of you aspiring politicians who are also creative types, resist the urge to go meta and have your audience miss your point. Particularly when you're running in a down-ballot, low voter turnout race, audience confusion can be deadly. Keep it simple. At its most basic, what you want is a noticeable logo that clearly informs the reader of your name and that doesn't make them want to barf.

If you lack artistic skills like me, don't be overly frugal – hire a designer. I found one on a website for freelance designers called Fiverr and paid less than 100 bucks for mine. I was lucky to find someone online who specialized in political logos, but if you have to pay more, you should. The last thing you want is to have a logo that screams amateurism. If your branding materials are subpar, people will question your competence. They'll impute any sloppiness, childishness, or silliness in your brand to you. You'll become your brand. Irella, for instance, had a logo that looked amateurish. I can't imagine it inspired confidence in potential voters. Your branding, on the other hand, can create an illusion that your campaign has more resources than it really does. Your logo in particular can help convey that you're a serious, legitimate contender for elected office. Avail yourself of this small but helpful advantage.

Your Look

Your brand is more than just letters and colors, though. When it comes down to it, your brand is you. You should thus give some thought to your choice of clothing, hygiene, hair, makeup, jewelry, the car you drive,[30] and so forth. There's no right or wrong here, per se. I hate shopping for clothes. And after several years in the military, I was sick of shaving every day. I also wear glasses. Buying a new wardrobe just seemed too vain, and my efforts at losing weight before the election plateaued. So, I just owned my "dadness" and wore jeans, running shoes, and a dress shirt when knocking on doors. I swapped out my jeans for slacks and my sneakers for dress shoes for events. For debates, it was a full suit and tie. Whatever look you choose, be consistent. This will help people recognize you and commit you and your candidacy to memory. For me, that meant shaving, getting rid of my high and tight, and keeping the glasses.

If you reflexively reject the idea that you should change your image to conform to stereotypes of how a politician should look, remember that we don't live in a perfect society. Residents will sometimes be brutally honest with you about how you look. On my first day of canvassing, I was so excited that I forgot to shave my face. An older gentleman took me to task for my look. In my head, I thought, "What a jerk!" But then I realized he had done me a favor. Other older voters would likely take offense to my five o'clock shadow and vote against me. I went home and got my razor. You can pout all day about superficiality, sexism, ageism, and other isms. At the end of the day, though, would you rather win your election, with all the opportunity for positive change that winning entails, or sit at home feeling indignant?

At the same time, make sure your brand taps into your truth. Don't just dress up how you expect a politician should look. If you're a single mother, don't throw your young-looking dad into your pictures, making it seem like he's your husband. Sounds gross, but I've seen it happen. Single dads: please don't convince your baby's mama to hold hands with you in photos. I've seen that too. You're forming a relationship with voters. The last thing you want is for that relationship to be based on falsehoods. Voters crave authenticity from their candidates and elected officials. Be your best self. But, above all, be your true self.

Your Pictures

Now that you're swathed in your preferred vestments, and you've straightened out your punim, you're going to need to be photographed. I wouldn't recommend a DIY approach here either unless you're a pro. And even then, you're limited in your ability to take good pictures of yourself as taking selfies makes you look immature. Most candidates hire a photographer to do a photo shoot for the website and for mailers. Our political consultant did our initial photography work, taking pictures of Christina, the kids, and me in front of the house and in our backyard. I felt silly, but the photos came out okay, despite the near 100-degree weather that day. He also had us take pictures at the local park with friends and supporters in attendance. The problem with these pictures is that they were staged and, therefore, unnatural. A better choice is to find a professional photog who will attend your events and take candid photos of you and your team. I found this person in one of my supporters, a local photographer named Rick Elias. Rick was among the most eccentric people I met during the campaign. Sporting silver-white hair and rocking a white Hummer, Rick owns a pink building in Uptown. Rick is hardcore about the need to remove all the Ficus trees, which stain the sidewalks with their figs.

I would give Rick a schedule of my goings-on: meet-and-greets, debates, alley cleanups, and so forth, and Rick would show up, take pictures, and send me the better ones for me to pick from. He would then touch them up for use on our website, on social media, or in mailers. Running for office is an experience that can produce moving, stressful, and even exuberant moments. By systematically capturing them, you let people into your world and help them get a better sense of who you are and why you're running. It allows people to know something about you that you can't convey with mere words.

Having a photographer follow you around might feel silly at first and may take some time getting comfortable with. Yet, it will ultimately save you a ton of time by incorporating picture-taking into your process. As with most of your campaign, quality control is vital. Using a smartphone camera isn't going to cut it because you'll need high-quality images that can be put into print.

Make sure you vet any picture before it goes public. I've seen candidates allow images of sign-in sheets with volunteers' addresses go online and other embarrassing photos making the rounds.

Your Website

You're likely going to have a distinct advantage over your older counterparts in the area of digital media. One such place where you can gain an advantage is your website. Your website is another way of showing you're the real deal. When serious voters, young or old, learn about the new, upstart candidate, the first thing they're going to do if they want to learn more is Google your name. If you don't have a website, if your website isn't easily accessible, or if your website is poorly designed, voters will quickly move on.

The first decision you need to make is what to name your website. If you haven't bought your name's web domain, stop whatever you're doing and do that right now. I purchased mine, authorhenrybouchot.com, using Google Domains, but there are other sites out there. It was cheap at $12 per year. This is just a no-brainer. Fail to do so and one of your opponents might just buy yours. The last thing you need is a website named after you with nothing but negative information. This happened to Texas Senator Ted Cruz and others.[31] You should also buy a few variations of your name. I bought henryforwhittier.com and henry-4whittier.com because I felt using my first name would put me on a regular, first-name basis with voters and because it was less clunky than something like www.henrybouchotforwhittiercity-council.com.

Next up, you should create an email address based on your website's name that forwards to your personal account. Voters will communicate with you via email, and you look like a tool when your email address is partyguy1989@hotmail.com. I bought www.forwhittier.com so I could ask people to email me at henry@for-whittier.com. If you have a common name like Bill Smith, you'll definitely want to buy a website domain like billsmithfortown-council.com. This will make it more likely that your name will come up in a Google search, although the quality and quantity of your website's content (and metadata) will affect that as well.

While on the subject of content, your website should probably include: an "about me" or biography section, a section for images and videos from the campaign, a "contact me" section, your platform, a disclaimer indicating that your political committee paid for the site, links to your social media sites, a donations page, and a calendar of events so that potential supporters can know when and where they can meet you in person. A blog is another option you should consider if you have the time. Include an endorsements section if local politicians or political groups have endorsed you – your memaw doesn't count, though, sorry.

Now, a word about design. At a minimum, your website should be simple, free from clutter, and accessible. By accessible, I mean, you should be able to find it online easily. If you're not a web designer, you can use WordPress, Squarespace, or any number of online web creation tools to set up something nice using a simple template. The trick is to have a good number of high-quality pictures, a high-res version of your logo, and to use your campaign colors in a consistent, thoughtful way. (So much of branding is consistency and restraint). You can create a superlative website by making sure it's intuitive, interactive, and frequently updated. To achieve that, though, you'll need help, and you'll need to think ahead. A web designer is your best bet for ensuring your layout makes sense. They will also ensure your site's user experience is intuitive and shows up in search.

Next up is your online biography. This is where your brand and strategy meet. It's who you are in the context of your campaign. Resist the urge to tell people anything and everything about you. Your bio is not your CV. It isn't an opportunity for you to repeat your platform, either. You want voters who read this section to get a basic mental snapshot of your life and career. Don't expect voters to choose you based on bio alone either, especially if you're running against an experienced politician. Below is what I used as my bio:

Henry Bouchot is an active member of our community. He and his wife, Christina, chose Whittier as their home to raise their two boys. A former Marine Captain who served in Afghanistan, Henry has a deep commitment to public service. He has served as a Whittier City Social Services Commissioner and currently serves as a Neighborhood Watch Block Captain.

Henry is the founder of a nonprofit organization dedicated to assisting disabled military veterans. He holds a law degree from Boston College and a master's degree in business from Mount Saint Mary's University. He earned a B.A. in history from Loyola Marymount University.

There are 77 words in this bio. And it invites more questions than it provides answers. This person is educated, but can he work with people? He's married with children. How long have they been married? How old are his kids? When did they move to Whittier? When did he serve in Afghanistan? What did he do there? By keeping it short, you pique the interest of the curious and provide those who are short of time with just enough information to make a decision. Save something for later. Unlike in large races where you have no hopes of meeting the vast majority of the electorate, you'll get an opportunity to convey to voters who you are in person.

When it comes to telling your story, it's essential to understand that good marketing works subconsciously. Hitting people over the head with your ideology or overdramatizing your story will never work as well as subtly conveying who you are and what you're about. Apple is an excellent example of a company that does this. All you need to know about their technology can be gleaned from its clean, sharp packaging. In this day and age, people are hyper-sensitive and hyper-partisan. They're eager to dismiss you as the other. You want to make sure you're getting past their defenses by coming across as a real person and not as a caricature.

A website, correctly done, should encourage your visitors to return for updates. For instance, I drafted a few blog posts throughout the campaign on issues relevant to residents. I then posted links to the blog posts on social media with a sentence or two encouraging readers to click through and read the full, long-form post.

While you'll likely spend more time on your social media efforts, don't ignore your website. Think of it as your home base. Use it to elaborate on positions in a way that would be ineffective in a social media context. Use your blog as an opportunity to work out some of your ideas in greater detail. This will communicate that you'll take your responsibilities seriously as an elected official. It'll help ward off accusations that you lack substance or don't know the issues.

Tagline

If a platform is what you use to convey the depth of your convictions to voters, then a tagline communicates what your campaign is about in a simple, memorable way. It's the tool you use to convey your campaign's theme as distinct from your platform. Locally, Bob went with "Proven Leadership," and Irella used "Experienced Leadership." For Bob, this made complete sense. After nine terms, it was hard to argue otherwise. Given the low esteem in which politicians are held nowadays, though, it's an open question just how praiseworthy a quality experience is exactly. Nowadays, "experience" is viewed as code for entrenched incumbent. Danny shot down my initial taglines, claiming they were too Obamaesque, meaning that I would come across as grandiose. I jokingly suggested going with "Give France a Chance" due to my French last name. The problem is that such humor would be lost on most. I ultimately settled on "Neighbor to Neighbor," which communicated the idea that this was a grassroots campaign.

Brainstorm catchy phrases that convey the essence of what the race is about. Ask yourself: What will voters say about the election once it's over? If Bob had won, people would have said, "Yep, the voters went with a proven leader." When I won, people said, "Henry ran a smart race, and he worked hard. He even went door to door, neighbor to neighbor." Distilling a campaign's essence into a catchphrase gives voters a heuristic, a simple mental trick for voters to remember you by. This is no small deal. Given the compressed nature of local campaigns, getting people to remember you is half the battle.

Swag

No one has ever been elected because they had the best pencils, bumper stickers, T-shirts, or buttons. And yet many candidates give in to their self-doubt and pay out the nose to purchase all manner of gewgaws and knickknacks. I suspect they do this to mask the inherent insecurity involved in competing in a race in which validation only comes at the end when they tally the votes. As I've discussed, money is at a premium in local races and must be spent carefully and effectively. Purchasing swag, unfortunately, is neither cost-effective nor persuasive. Better to save your cash for the essentials.

Of course, there are exceptions to the rule, and here are mine. If you're running an effective campaign, you'll be hosting several events and interacting with the public at various locations. It's always good to have something to give away to promote your campaign. Bumper stickers aren't a useful tool as they spend most of their time commuting in other cities, or in the garage. Shirts are fun but cost-prohibitive. Practically any other object not commonly associated with political campaigns – pencils, playing cards, or ponchos – threatens to make your campaign seem jokey. Buttons, on the other hand, are a well-accepted form of political advertising. They're small, affordable, and stand out. Get yourself a whole bunch and pass them out to supporters.

I also had business cards made with my campaign email address and a phone number I set up just for the campaign. If, like me, you didn't grow up in the place in which you're running, your area code might draw suspicion. In that case, you might want to reach out to your mobile phone carrier, as I did, and have them add a number to your account with your town's area code. This'll help you avoid looking like an out-of-towner. It'll also allow you to give out your number freely, conveying your accessibility without worrying about compromising your long-term personal number. Pens are good too in that the recipient might use it more than once.

When you participate in candidate forums, the host usually allows candidates to set up whatever materials they have outside the debate hall. You would do good to invest in a brochure, a neat display setup, and even a small table that breaks down quickly. This way, you can convey your professionalism to potential voters. It's not essential – Irella and Eric did this, and it didn't win them the election – but it's a nice touch.

As I neared the election, I met with a couple of college friends for dinner. One was a local artist, and she mentioned that I needed to "cutesify" my campaign. It was true that there wasn't much that was flashy about my branding. As a former Marine, "cute" isn't the look I'm usually going for. I also felt trying to be cute would seem fake. The more I thought about it though, the more I realized she was right. I was missing an opportunity, as a young candidate, to come across as youthful. I was grateful she had brought this to my attention.

I figured nothing says, "I'm a young, fun alternative" candidate than associating myself with the arts. The most artsy area in my district is in the Uptown area. Teens, young families, and artists go there for food, drinks, and play, especially during our monthly Art Walk. So, I commissioned a poster of me to put up on the Uptown storefronts. It mimicked the famous Obama "Hope" posters but used my color scheme and changed out "Hope" for "Vote" with the election date written at the bottom. We put the signs up a week or two before the election and waited. Whether it helped, I can't say for sure. However, it was a creative way to show that Whittier would get "a new, fresh look" and that I was "the new face" in Whittier politics.

Endorsements

There's a saying that goes, "Show me your friends, and I'll tell you who you are." Endorsements work in much the same way. You and your endorsers become intertwined in the eyes of the public. Endorsements give the public a shorthand understanding of who you are since voters assume you share your endorsers' values. This is why I decided not to ask former California State Senator Tony Mendoza for an endorsement when credible allegations surfaced that he had sexually harassed his interns and staffers.

There's another reason to tread lightly where endorsements are concerned. Endorsements are a tricky business given the egos involved. Refusing to ask for one or, worse yet, refusing one after it has been offered, can transform a passive endorser into an active one – for your opponent. Don't get offended if you don't get the endorsements you want as a dark horse candidate, either. Look at the endorsement process not solely from your point of view but from that of the endorser. Choosing wrong as an incumbent can mean creating powerful enemies, an incumbents win most of the time.

If you do get endorsements, don't expect them to win the election for you. Sometimes you can get a token endorsement out of a sense of obligation, to repay a favor, or because there's no other option. Usually, this means you get to use the endorser's name on campaign literature but not much else: no personal appearances, fundraising assistance, or help mustering volunteers. What you really want is a full-throated endorsement with all the fixings. However, that only tends to happen when there is a pre-existing relationship or a strategic benefit to the endorser. If you're a newcomer to the game, you'll likely get unenthusiastic endorsements at best.

If you're lucky, you might receive lots of endorsements. There's a downside to this: you may be seen as the establishment candidate. This happened to Bob. He secured the endorsement of practically every local elected official, Democrat or Republican, before I even had a chance to reach out to them. His list of representatives, senators, assembly members, county supervisors, councilpersons, and school board members was a mile long. It was so long that it likely hurt his chances of reelection as it screamed status quo at a time when change was in the offing.

Politicians aren't the only source of political endorsements. There are also plenty of organizations that endorse candidates in local races. These include your regional political party and its local affiliate chapters, labor unions, and special interest groups of all stripes. If you're active in a political party, a member of a union or a trade group, or at least have some connection to them, it would behoove you to seek their support.

I fared somewhat better when it came to the organizational endorsements than I did with politician endorsements. Bob had the business community's support through the Los Angeles County Business Federation plus the Whittier Conservancy. Irella, meanwhile, had the help of the local teachers' union. And so, there I was, no name recognition, no labor support, no love from the liberal activists, no endorsements from any of the politicians, and no help from the business community or labor unions. There's a reason my father's tombstone reads, "Never, never, never give up." It's our family mantra. When times get hard, we dig in and find a way.

In Bob's case, I pulled a judo move. I turned his endorsements into a positive for me, playing up the fact that they only showed how heavily the odds were stacked in his favor. In me, I explained, voters had a chance to tell these elitists who really was in charge. Irella, meanwhile, had the misfortune of Lizette, the Democrat running in District 4, receiving $20,000 in donation from organized labor all in one lump sum just as Irella was receiving the bulk of her labor union donations. Thus, while the *Whittier Daily News* article on the first campaign finance deadline was about how much the mayor and I had jumped out to a lead in our races,[32] the second article was phrased as labor unions outside the city's limits attempting to influence the race. The newspaper insinuated that it was for less than altruistic reasons. This made my independence an asset. Because I had avoided endorsement-related entanglements, I watched the drama that ensued from a safe distance, unscathed by the crossfire.

My opponents proved that endorsements have their limitations and downsides and that discretion is ultimately crucial even when it comes to them. Just as in other aspects of campaigning, the law of diminishing returns applies to endorsements. There's always a possibility of a backlash when trying to deprive your opponent of support by cornering the endorsements market.

In the end, I ended up getting a few key endorsements, including from the local college newspaper,[33] a former state senator living in the city, a county library commissioner, and a local community college board member who also recorded a robocall for me. My endorsements came as a result of my hard work and performance rather than my political connections. Endorsers came to my side when they saw that I had a shot at winning and that I was outperforming my opponents in candidate forums, fundraising, and canvassing. Their support helped give me the credibility and legitimacy necessary to get voters to provide me with a closer look.

Best of all, I avoided the drama, handwringing, and, most of all, the excessive time involved in securing endorsements. In the end, most endorsements are marginally helpful anyway, particularly in the present political climate, when being an insider or part of the establishment is frowned upon. And the more you have to work for them, especially mid-campaign, the less time you have for the nitty-gritty activity of winning an election. (There's a reason I put this topic in the section on branding and not on earning votes). Do yourself a favor and think critically about which endorsements you want, which endorsements you need, and which endorsements you can get. Going willy-nilly after any and all endorsements is only bound to make you miserable given the personalities, and games, involved.

The one endorsement you should care about, no matter what, is the endorsement of your political party. Even if the chances of getting it are slim, you must seek it out because the benefits are significant, even despite relatively diminishing party influence. Whereas obtaining endorsements from politicians is mostly informal, with the most challenging part being finding a way to get in contact and scheduling an interview, the party endorsement is usually a multi-phase process with a local interview, questionnaires, and potentially a speech at the county party meeting.

Irella had had a forgettable performance in our first candidate forum by the time I had a chance to get in front of my party's local endorsement subcommittee. In contrast, I had handled myself well by most accounts. My involvement in local politics, starting with the 2016 election, paved the way for the delegates to recommend me for endorsement by the Los Angeles County Democratic Party (LACDP). Still, much was up in the air. I would need 60% of the votes to receive their blessing. Irella would presumably have union support and it wasn't at all clear that the party would reject a long-serving Democrat (Bob) endorsed by practically every local elected official.

In the end, preparation and luck played critical roles in my reeling in the big one. Bob sat the interview out. Irella made a couple of faux pas during her interview. She neglected to get the "union bug," a logo denoting the use of a unionized printer, on the business cards she handed to the interviewers. She also failed to familiarize herself with hydraulic fracturing, also known as fracking. Switching her registration to Independent and back to Democrat just in time for the election didn't help her cause either. I received all the subcommittee's votes save for one. Later, I secured the county party's endorsement, arriving in person to make sure neither Irella nor Bob stole it at the eleventh hour with an impassioned speech.

While the race was a nonpartisan one, meaning that party preference wouldn't be listed on the ballot, I used this endorsement to significant effect. I sent out a mailer with the LACDP logo to households with only registered Democrats touting myself as the lone Democrat in the race endorsed by the party. Whatever legitimacy Bob and Irella worked so hard to deny me, I gained back by working hard and showing I had a great chance of winning. This, in turn, gave the party delegates the confidence to provide me with the party endorsement.

One last endorsement that proved to be of some consequence to me was that of the League of Conservation Voters, an environmental advocacy group. It came with money, the best type of endorsement. More importantly, it related to something I care about, preserving the environment, and fit within my overall strategy since I opposed drilling in the Whittier Hills.

Ultimately, while he had more of them than me, Bob's

endorsements said, "I've been in politics a long time." Irella's meanwhile conveyed, "I've made powerful allies." Before you get involved in the effort and drama that are endorsements, know your strategy, and that of your opponents, and target endorsers wisely. Make sure your endorsements are "on brand." Discretion, after all, is the better part of valor.

Kicking Off the Campaign

So, you now know how much you need to raise and spend, and you might've even started to raise some cash. You have the beginnings of a brand, perhaps an endorsement or two, and you're ready to put your best face forward. You feel good, and you want to kick your campaign off in some meaningful way. So, what do you do? As I mentioned above, most do something along the lines of a kickoff fundraiser or pep rally. I would recommend foregoing the rally. You're not Obama or Bernie. Leave convention-style events to the heavy hitters. What's more, such events tend to draw out looky-loos who come for the food but don't stick around for the work.

You could draft a press release, but the decline in local newspaper coverage makes it unlikely that it'll be picked up as newsworthy enough for an article of its own. You could pay to have the press release published in the local newspaper, I suppose. Your money is probably better preserved for when more eyeballs are focused on the race, which comes later down the road as the election nears.

More and more lately, it seems that the big announcement comes by way of a Facebook post. It's not a terrible way to go as it gives your online followership a bump. My Facebook announcement post garnered 150 or so followers from my own Facebook friends. This helped jump-start my public social media profile. The extra followers came in handy when raising funds online and getting the word out about my goings-on and events. For me, the question wasn't so much how to announce but when.

I felt pressure starting in September 2017, over six months before the race, when Irella began posting heavily to the Next-Door app. NextDoor is a social networking site for neighbors that focuses primarily on local nuisances and public safety issues. Matters like lost dogs, residential burglaries, police pursuits, noise, litter, and utility bill questions are commonly posted to NextDoor. Irella started to leverage her position as a neighborhood "lead" to post about art-related activity and to promote education-related issues.

While her written posts weren't the most cogent, she was getting her name out, sending emoji-laden messages to dozens of communities in the district and sometimes throughout the city. When she announced she was having a meet-and-greet, I worried I might be falling behind.

My plan all along had been to announce in January, about three months before the April election, to preserve as much of an element of surprise as possible. Now, I wondered how long I could fly under the radar without becoming an afterthought. Frankly, I was also looking for some measure of reassurance and relief. I was like a boxer ready to come out of the corner swinging.

I thus acted reactively by announcing my candidacy online a few days after Irella's meet-and-greet. Ultimately, relief comes only on election night. Whether you announce three months or a year before, what matters is that you're prepared to run your best campaign during the ten or so weeks when campaign season is in full gear. At the end of the day, Irella wasn't and I was. Her spamming the entire city didn't amount to much in the grand scheme of things. Neither did my jumping the gun and announcing early, though. Announce when you're good and ready and when it feels right, and no earlier.

Honestly, the *real* start of the campaign happens when you start canvassing. That means the best way to kick off a campaign is to make it a canvassing event. Canvassing can be laborious and unglamorous. Make it fun by having supporters over for breakfast and a short speech and then get everyone outside for some door knocking. There's no sense in riling people up just to have their energy go nowhere. Put your people to good use. Put them to work.

SUMMARY

- ∧ To run for office is to sell (yourself). Effective branding does the selling for you.
- ∧ Run on local, not federal issues. Explain why you're well-suited to fix these issues. Offer new, practical solutions. Know what you're talking about.
- ∧ Tap into feelings with your platform. Know what people worry about, what they hope for.
- ∧ Voter concerns change. Anticipate emerging issues.
- ∧ Design a simple logo but not an amateurish one.
- ∧ Be authentically you.
- ∧ Professionally photograph your events.
- ∧ Buy your website domain now.
- ∧ Pique voter interest with your biography.
- ∧ Incorporate a blog into your website.
- ∧ A tagline can help voters remember you.
- ∧ Don't buy unnecessary swag.
- ∧ Endorsements are tricky. Proceed with caution.
- ∧ Don't waste your time on a big campaign kickoff event unless it's also a fundraiser or a canvassing event.

RESOURCES

For additional sample platforms and bios, candidate logo and website examples, pictures from our campaign, and a deep dive into the party endorsement process, please visit authorhenrybouchot.com.

CHAPTER 12

THE BATTLE OF THE BALLOT

When and how you announce your campaign is much less important than ensuring you get on the ballot in the first place. I touched on the process of getting on the ballot in the section on managing your political consultant. Suffice to say that you need to be intimately familiar with the detailed rules for getting on the ballot. When in doubt, consult with the local election official, usually the city clerk or the county registrar-recorder. Be careful about getting assistance gathering signatures because there are rules about who can help you gather them. In California, for example, gatherers must sign an affidavit. Don't be lackadaisical and make a fatal mistake, like falling one signature short of the requirement. Your opponents may pounce on you, as I was ready to do when Irella nearly missed the filing deadline. Don't put your electoral fate in the hands of your rivals. The opportunity to knock your opponent out of the race on a technicality is simply too tempting. Start early, get more than enough signatures, submit them on time, and obtain written confirmation that you did it correctly. You can never be too careful.

Ballot Description

Assuming you successfully get on the ballot, the next major decision will be what ballot description to use. This is no small matter. So-called down-ballot races are typically low turnout and low information. This means the average voter gives these races little thought and frequently chooses based on name, party preference, and ballot designation.

Races for judge in California, for example, which are even further down the ballot than city council or school board races, frequently turn into legal battles about whether a prosecutor was in the gang or domestic violence unit long enough to be labeled a "Gang Prosecutor" or "Domestic Violence Prosecutor." Public Defenders running in conservative districts frequently go with "Attorney at Law" because of the stigma some associate with representing criminal defendants. For all your efforts, success or defeat can hinge on a single word.

Typically, you're only allowed a short designator. There are detailed rules for what you can use thanks to all the yokels who've tried to call themselves Sensei, Grand Puba, or whatever. Basically, your designation has to be something you do professionally and cannot be an adjective or a descriptor. Your designation can't be "Veteran" or "Community Activist" any more than it could be "Warrior" or "Intellectual."

There are also rules regarding using the word "retired" and using the term "incumbent." Appointed councilpersons in California, for instance, can't call themselves incumbents. There are also esoteric rules about hyphenation and word counts. Typically, three words are the limit, but you can get around this limit if the words would naturally be hyphenated or if the position's name is longer than three words. This was the case with Irella, a member of the "Whittier City Elementary School Board of Trustees." The coupling of titles is allowed so long as the rules surrounding brevity are abided by. Usually, the titles are separated by a slash. Since my race was the first race under the new district system, technically, Bob wasn't an incumbent. Fortunately, it didn't become an issue in the race as he chose "Councilperson / Insurance Salesman." That was a good thing for me because candidates must self-regulate, and you want to avoid coming across as litigious or petty.

Frankly, I thought Bob made a mistake referring to himself as an insurance salesman on the ballot. I researched and discovered that insurance salespeople are among the few positions held in lower esteem than lawyers, which I am by trade. As you might expect, police officers and firefighters are held in the highest regard in America. You'll likely have several options based on your profession and volunteer activities. Before you register, ask yourself how your designation stacks up to that of your competitors. It's okay to embellish here within reason. Think of Disneyland. You aren't Goofy there; you're a "Cast Member."

Think your ballot designation through carefully. Pick something that helps you stand out, and be ready to defend your choice, especially if you're in career transition, as many young, mid-career professionals frequently are. Above all, don't take the ballot designation lightly. Do your research and be careful, as you'll be an attractive target as a young up-and-comer.

Ballot Order

I mentioned Tony Mendoza and his sexual harassment scandal earlier. He dug his heels in, denying the allegations, but eventually capitulated, resigning from the state senate rather than risk being expelled. [34] Instead of riding off into the sunset, though, he ran for both the special election to complete his unfinished term and the regular election for the ensuing four years. He lost, placing fourth in both. However, something incredibly interesting happened in the process. Vanessa Delgado, a real estate developer who served on the Montebello city council at the time, won the special election for the remaining months of Mendoza's term. When it came to the more important race for the four-year term, she placed second, shockingly. The winner was Bob Archuleta, an Army veteran and former Pico Rivera councilman.

Archuleta was little known outside of his hometown, raised less money than the competition, and lacked the Democratic Party's support. Someone even ran attack ads with his head on an elephant, calling him a DINO. However, Bob had the luck of the gods, having drawn a ballot order with his name placed first in the race for the four-year term. Statistically, being listed first on the ballot is best, last is second-best, and being stuck in the middle is worst. First place is most advantageous in races with a long list of candidates and relatively low voter interest. Why the state doesn't go to randomized ballots is unclear to me. (California has gone to an electronic voting system where, supposedly, the ballot order is less of a determining factor than it used to be with each race getting its own page).

So, what does this mean for your race? Pray for first and have a plan for everything else. In my race, I was last with Eric Leckey being first. Bob, Irella, and Vincent McLeod were sandwiched in the middle. While being first would have been ideal, I avoided the misfortune of having Bob get first with me caught in the middle. That would have been incredibly difficult to overcome, compounding my lack of name identification compared to Bob. That didn't mean I was out of the woods. A bubble followed my name closely with a line next to it for write-in candidates. When you have busy ballots with lots of text on them, the room for confusion is high. About a hundred voters in my race selected the write-in candidate bubble, with most leaving out a name, presumably intending to vote for me. In a way, I ran against five other candidates: Bob, Irella, Eric, Vince, and "Mr./Ms. Enter Write-In Candidate Here."

If you do get a worst-case scenario ballot order, don't just hope for a miracle. Discuss it with your political consultant and work out scenarios where you can still win the race. Revise your numbers (to include the amount of mail you'll send and doors you'll hit) to offset the disadvantage. Give yourself an extra margin of error, increase your fundraising goals, and seek out additional volunteers. Try to leave as little as you can to the luck of the draw.

Ballot Statement

The next critical ballot-related task is the ballot statement. A good number of voters will decide whom to vote for based on these statements. You don't get a ton of space, so you have to make every word count. While most candidate statements have an obligatory biographical paragraph, your statement is not your biography. If done well, it will tell a story about you, the community, and the election. This isn't the place to be subtle or self-effacing. There's just not enough space for subtlety. Your statement should grab the reader from the beginning and hold their attention to the end.

My statement started with the ominous sounding, "For too long, Whittier residents have been left to fend for themselves while City Hall stands by as crime plagues their neighborhoods and traffic chokes their streets." In retrospect, I was overly apocalyptic. You don't want to throw the baby out with the bathwater when it comes to your city. Having reviewed Bob's previous statements, though, I knew he would paint an overly rosy picture of a Mayberry community that was no longer jibing with residents' perceptions. While I was embellishing, my point was to drive home to voters the urgency of the situation.

My next goal was to emphasize the most significant difference between my opponents and me, my independence: "Regular people finally have a chance to select a representative who will fight for their interests, not for oil companies, political elites, or developers." Sure, I was calling my opponents out on the carpet with this shot across the bow, but, as they say, nothing ventured, nothing gained. (Yep, that was a cliché trifecta). The point is you must paint a compelling picture and not merely sketch out your bio or list your platform in bullet point format. That approach is a lazy way to bore voters into choosing someone else.

Before finishing your statement, make sure to actually overtly ask for a vote. I combined my ask with a summation of my platform: "Vote for me, and I will implement a plan to increase safety, reduce congestion, revitalize Uptown, and alleviate homelessness. The time for a change is now. Join me. Together we can bring about that change and create a better Whittier." Include your email address and campaign phone number. It's an easy way to convey your approachability.

If you live in a place with a substantial number of foreign-language speakers, pay to have your statement translated. It's worth the investment. Just make sure you have a native speaker look over the translation. Ensure the official translation is faithful to your English version's tone, verbiage, and syntax.

Ballot Name

Most of you will simply use whatever name is on your birth certificate on the ballot. In California and in other places, this isn't strictly necessary. As you may recall, candidate Deez Nuts received third place in the North Carolina presidential primary in 2016. (No, I'm not making this up). I wouldn't suggest you emulate Mr. Nuts. However, there are some instances when using something other than your birth name might make sense. I have a friend who goes by his stepfather's last name. His stepfather raised him. Unlike his stepfather's name, his birth name is Hispanic, and he lives in a heavily Latino area. If he ever runs for office, he'll be faced with a tough choice.

As elsewhere in campaigning, avoid gimmicks. Don't run as Joe "No More Taxes" Blow. Don't make up an ethnic-sounding name just because you think it'll help you win. The one odd name change I have seen work successfully was former Los Angeles Mayor Antonio Villaraigosa. He was born Antonio Villar and married a woman with the last name of Raigosa. I'm not sure when or why he combined the names, but the combination did have a nice ring to it and seems to have helped him stand out.

Party Preference

The numbers indicate that the party system is declining in America. Once, the parties had a death grip on the electorate. Now, you hear of candidates from formerly fringe groups like the Democratic Socialists of America pulling out elections against long-time incumbents. The number of "no party preference" voters is rapidly rising, particularly among the young. With people feeling disgusted with leaders from both major political parties, more and more voters are registering as Independents (or "Decline to State" as it's called here in California).

Like many others, I registered as an Independent when I first turned 18. That was around the time of the 2000 presidential election when there was a great deal of frustration about the perception that Republicans and Democrats were too similar. (Seems like a long time ago now). Although I was swept up in the 2008 presidential race while in law school at Boston College, attending the Boston rally where Massachusetts Senator Ted Kennedy endorsed Obama, I didn't register as a Democrat until after I was honorably discharged from the Marines in 2015.

While the parties may be declining, partisan affinity, sometimes referred to as "lean," hasn't. This means most voters associate with one party or the other on a cultural level, whether or not they formally register with any particular party. Life is complicated, and many voters don't have the luxury of deeply researching each candidate for office, their platforms, and backgrounds. This is particularly true in California where hundreds of municipalities form a patchwork quilt of government responsibility (or irresponsibility). Voters use party preference as a heuristic for simplifying a difficult choice.

If you register Independent, you're essentially confusing voters, making them wonder who you are and what you're about. Go with your conscience if you're genuinely an Independent but be honest with yourself and make sure you're not merely rebelling without a cause. Whereas registering as a Democrat will cause Republicans to write you off and registering as a Republican will cause Democrats to forego you, Independent status means voters from both of the major parties will ignore you.

But what, you ask, if that means running against the establishment candidate for your party and the hate and discontent that it will cause? (I'm assuming, of course, that there's no primary system in your jurisdiction). Party leaders will accuse you of working at cross-purposes, of fighting the wrong enemy. I understand their frustration, but democracy relies on competition and transparency to function correctly. Americans have historically rejected entrenched political elites. Perpetual incumbencies weaken our political system as increasingly entitled politicians take the privilege of holding office for granted. As they say in the Marines, comfort kills. Bob warned that voting for someone other than him could lead to Whittier becoming like Bell, a city known for its past political corruption. It's been a while since I was elected, and Whittier hasn't gone off the rails. To borrow another phrase from the Marines, no one's irreplaceable.

At the same time, think of the consequences and don't just rush in blindly. In Whittier, two Democrats ran in each of the three 2020 races, districts 1, 3, and the mayor's race, splitting up the vote. All six Democrats lost, leading to a Republican supermajority on the council in a city where almost two-thirds of registered voters are Democrats.

Party preference won't be an official consideration in those local races that are technically nonpartisan. In these elections, the ballot will lack any indication of political party preference, the idea being that local politics shouldn't reflect the partisan nature of state or federal government. (It's often said that potholes aren't partisan). The reality is different. Informed voters tend to know what general ideological lines candidates fall within, especially when it comes to incumbents. However, in races with multiple candidates, voters might not realize to which party a given candidate belongs.

I was able to use this to my advantage. Partly, this was out of necessity. My principal opponents were Democrats. Without name recognition or strong party support, I'd have to assemble a coalition that included voters from left, right, and center. Not having to disclose my party preference on the ballot allowed me to get by the immediate defensiveness that comes with party tribalism and let voters get to know me, and what I stand for, before making their decisions. If you're in a nonpartisan race, think long and hard before publicly declaring yourself a hardcore partisan. Doing so means potentially leaving votes on the table. Another benefit of eschewing partisan labels: you get to know a broader cross-section of your constituency, which helps you govern after you win. Of course, this doesn't prevent you from signaling your shared party affiliation to voters through targeted messaging as I'll discuss in the following chapters.

SUMMARY

- The ballot is a potential source of strategic advantage. Choose wisely.
- Get creative (within reason) with your ballot designation.
- Hope for first on the ballot order but have a plan for other scenarios.
- Tell voters a compelling story through your ballot statement.
- Strive to represent all voters regardless of party affiliation.

RESOURCES

For additional examples of ballot statements, research on ballot order, links to stories about court battles over ballot descriptions, and more please check out authorhenrybouchot.com.

CHAPTER 13

VOTER TARGETING

Before you run off and start making contact with voters, you should first pinpoint those subsections of the voting population that offer the greatest return on investment, vote for vote. Campaigning is about selectivity. You never use a hammer when a scalpel will do. There simply aren't enough resources to go around – in any race but especially not at the local level – for you to blanket the populace. Each race will involve a different set of voters. Still, the following discussion should give you an idea of the analysis you must undertake when deciding who to put in the pool of voters potentially sympathetic to you, the so-called "voter universe."

Party Affiliation

The first source of potential voters may be apparent. You'll tend to put a greater emphasis on voters from your own political party. This isn't about encouraging partisanship. It's merely a recognition of the mathematical realities of campaigning. Working within the parameters of a partisan electorate is different from fanning partisan flames. Focusing on the members of your political party first, whether in a partisan or nonpartisan race, is a necessity (as they're the most likely to support you). You'll probably need to set aside your desire to be a consensus candidate in a one-on-one race between a Democrat and a Republican and do your best to get out your own vote. Spread yourself too thin, trying to hit all voters, and you'll dilute your resources, inadvertently depreciating the voters most likely to support you. If, and only if, you have extra resources, should you reach out to voters from across the aisle.

Gender

Increasingly, and rightfully so, voters are seeking greater gender equality in their legislatures. If you plan on making your gender a focal point of the campaign, consider how to frame it so as to obtain the maximum share of votes possible. While the idea that gender is an automatic qualifier for office might seem manifest to you, don't assume voters will automatically agree. Keep in mind that voters primarily consider the WIFM – what's in it for me. They aren't mainly interested in helping you become the first anything.

High Propensity Voters

Basic human psychology tells us that past behavior is a good predictor of future actions. This means that the five-in-five voter is more likely to cast a ballot than the four-in-five voter and so on. Logic tells us that targeting the five-in-five voter is more effective than the one-in-five voter or the none-in-five voter.

The problem is that training all your resources on people who are already predisposed to vote tends to perpetuate the status quo. Because the poor and the young (minorities too) are statistically more likely to sit out elections, those elected tend to represent the will of the older and wealthier voters who put them in office. And so, the poor stay poor, and the young get saddled with debt. I don't know about you, but I hate the idea of perpetuating this cycle. The dilemma you face as a candidate is that focusing exclusively on low propensity voters is typically a recipe for failure. Nonetheless, you have a responsibility as a leader to buck a system that benefits the few over the many.

Here's how I addressed this challenge. At first, I focused exclusively on the first tier of high propensity voters – those who vote in every election. In time, by knocking on doors every weekend, and eventually every day, I reached a point where I couldn't knock on any more high propensity voters' doors without experiencing diminishing returns. I then moved to progressively lower propensity voters. I also used social media to reach voters in a more democratic way than canvassing (since Facebook doesn't allow you to target using voting patterns). As my campaign grew and I received more donations, I set aside resources for lower propensity voters, and you should do so too.

Neighborhoods

I covered demographics earlier when I discussed setting policy goals that would resonate with voters based on demographic factors such as income, language, country of origin, ethnicity, and so on. Now, the task is to "reverse engineer" your platform and nail down where these discrete groups of people, known in elections parlance as "communities of interest," you'll need drive out can be found. That'll help you allocate your canvassing time.

Daniel, an urban planning graduate, helped me analyze our local demographics. Daniel looked at the census data and took away some key findings (as paraphrased by me):

1. We have a source of untapped support in the northwest area near the 605 freeway and the area around

Palm Park, both stable, middle-class neighborhoods consisting of second-generation Latinos.

2. Uptown disguises as middle class, with its historic homes, but actually experiences significant income inequality and is composed primarily of renters, making the neighborhood up for grabs.

3. The hills are older, whiter, and more affluent. As such, they'll likely skew toward Henderson. Still, there might be an opening among those who oppose oil drilling.

Armed with this knowledge, I now knew that to win, I would need a landslide victory among the middle-class Latino residents of Palm Park and Northwest Whittier. I would also need to tie in Uptown, where votes from low propensity, apartment dwellers could help me offset losses among the house dwelling, high-propensity preservationist Bob supporters there. If I could make the race competitive in the affluent hills, that would be a bonus. My chances of winning depended on my ability to know who was more likely to vote for me and where to find them. This knowledge dramatically altered the way I allocated resources during the campaign, allowing me to shift my emphasis to areas such as Palm Park and carefully choose which canvassers to send to which neighborhoods (and how often to send them).

In sum, make sure it's "ready, aim, fire," not "fire, ready, aim" when it comes to identifying the electorate. Don't assume you know who your voters are just because you've lived in a community. No matter how large your social network, it's likely only a tiny slice of your local voting population.

SUMMARY

- ^ You can't reach out to every single voter in most jurisdictions. There just aren't enough resources to go around.
- ^ Start by targeting members of your own political party.
- ^ Focus on high propensity voters, but not exclusively.
- ^ Find out where your voters are and go to them.

RESOURCES

For a more in-depth analysis of how to access voter data, locate your voters, and whether and how to group voters by ethnicity, age, or other identifying characteristics, please visit authorhenrybouchot.com.

CHAPTER 14

EARNING VOTES AT THE DOOR

You can do *everything* I've suggested up to this point and still lose. In politics, flexibility and perseverance are just as important as proper planning. As the Marines say, no plan survives first contact with the enemy. (Mike Tyson might have put it best when he said: "Everybody has a plan until they get punched in the mouth"). Go out there and earn your votes. Don't whine or complain when things go wrong. Just win.

A campaign isn't a contest of resumes but a battle of wills. Sometimes your strategy is to grind down your opponent, pitting your will against theirs. Even when your strategy is not attrition-ary, your commitment to winning will still be critical in pulling out a victory. They call it a *race* for a reason. Once the period for getting on the ballot closes and you're officially a candidate, it's a literal race to the finish. Take nothing for granted. To win, you'll need to run hard and run through the finish line.

There'll be moments when you'll be tested. An opponent will get under your skin. Your closest supporters will make you look bad. A resident will be rude to you at their door. Someone might even threaten you. No matter how laid-back you might be, the race will test your willpower, composure, and possibly your integrity.

This combination of fear and competitiveness arguably got the best of Larry Haendiges. Larry won a seat on the Whittier City Council in 1992 only to withdraw after it came to light that he had stabbed himself and filed a false police report during the campaign. Larry had apparently been receiving threatening voicemails.[35] Mind yourself and avoid uncivil or overzealous behavior. Local government is one of the last remaining bastions of responsive government left, literally keeping the lights on and the water running. Put your community first and keep your honor clean.

There will also be joyful moments. While campaigning is in some ways akin to running a business, it doesn't have to be *all* business. Look at your campaign as an opportunity to be in communion with your fellow neighbors. I'm not talking about religion here, but there is an element of campaigning that is transcendent. A campaign is special because it allows you to get close to people who were once strangers, transforming them into neighbors, friends, and even family.

Canvassing 101

Before we get into the art of talking-the-talk, there are two lessons you need to learn about soliciting votes, also known as canvassing or voter canvassing. First, although it's the most laborious and time-consuming method of vote-getting, it's also the most productive. There's a certain "stickiness" to showing up at someone's door and asking for a vote that doesn't exist with other types of messaging. That's probably because other kinds of communication are one-sided. When you receive a mailer, you quickly digest the message – if you bother to look at all – and you move on with your life. There's no commitment involved. A face-to-face conversation that ends with a promise to vote for a candidate is a social contract, a pact. Many people take their vote incredibly seriously, as they should, and getting their vote doesn't come easy. But once you get it, they'll be with you through the end. Thus, in-person solicitation will be the foundation of any winning campaign.

The second basic idea is that a candidate's knock is worth a lot more than anyone else's. Your volunteers, no matter how enthusiastic or well trained, usually aren't going to beat you in effectiveness door-for-door. So, you can give up any illusions of hanging back at campaign headquarters, overseeing a crew of campaigners from afar. Like a quarterback on a scramble, directing your blockers and receivers on the fly while gobbling up field, you need to lead from the front.

When I noticed that I was spending too much time getting my volunteers ready and out the door, I completely revamped my process. I prepared bags with the necessary materials and placed them where recurring volunteers would find them. I left one person behind to onboard any new volunteers, and out the door I went. My time was too critical for me to remain at campaign headquarters (our house).

If you as the candidate are 1A in terms of your value at the door, your significant other, if you have one, is 1B. Christina, in many ways, was a better canvasser than me. She's a great listener and has a nonjudgmental, understanding aura to her. She graciously offered to take a couple of weeks off from work before the election to knock on doors full-time. If your significant other is equally committed, consider yourself lucky and thank him or her profusely. Kids, on the other hand, are a different manner. I took our four-year-old son John with me once, thinking he might have some fun, but poor John asked to come home within maybe three blocks. Better leave the little ones at home – for their own good and yours.

Volunteers

If you had a year or more to canvass every day, you might be able to tackle an election all by yourself. The reality is that there's only a short window during which voters will welcome your solicitations, and you have to make the best use of this time, which means relying on volunteers. Not all volunteers are created equal, though. And some can actually be harmful to your cause. Your volunteers are an extension of you. If they're ill-informed, pushy, rude, or obnoxious, you can bet voters will assume you are too. Quality control and effective onboarding are thus key. Early on in your campaign, you'll be desperate for volunteers. Still, don't take on just anyone.

One way of implementing quality control on the fly is to take volunteers out with you canvassing. I had a rule that a canvasser couldn't go out alone without on-the-job training with either me or with an experienced canvasser first. This had multiple benefits. It allowed me to observe each volunteer in a live setting. This permitted me to make sure they were taking it seriously and weren't going to make me look bad. It also allowed me to familiarize the volunteer with my platform, delivery, and style. Unfortunately, too many campaigns provide little to no training other than a dull script that the volunteer is expected to read aloud. The problem is that watching someone read from a script is painfully awkward and also really annoying when you have a pot on the stove or a shower running.

You should also do your best to make sure you're able to receive volunteers warmly and show you appreciate their time. Make sure someone is there to greet your volunteers when they arrive, thank them warmly for their time, and provide them with food and drink. From there, take the time to supervise and train each volunteer until they get a handle. While this takes some upfront effort, it pays off in the end because they'll get the thrill of convincing voters to support change, and you'll get a repeat volunteer.

When the volunteer is done, take the time to debrief and thank him or her. Canvassing is fun when you're dabbling. As a volunteer canvasser, you're excited to be out there. You want to feel you did something good for society, and you're keen on sharing your war stories afterward. Let them. It'll make them more likely to return. Anecdotal evidence is imperfect, of course, but it does help suss out what the numbers say, providing them with real-life, flesh-and-blood contour.

Campaigning is an iterative, trial-and-error process. You interact with the community, the voters learn about you, and they communicate back how they feel about you. Your task is to take what voters are saying, process that information, and incorporate it into your campaign. In my case, voters kept saying, "We need new blood," "We need a fresh face on the council," or "Bob has stayed on too long." Even Bob's longtime supporters were receptive to a change in leadership. That told me people were okay with hearing from someone who could offer a sharp contrast to the old regime. Perhaps if my opponents had been listening more closely to the voters and their willingness to critique Bob, they might've been less deferential to him.

Frankly, the hardest part of dealing with volunteers is finding new ones. Your volunteers will thus almost certainly be your closest friends, family, and sometimes your work colleagues.

Preferably, they'll be from the local community since it's hard to be convinced to vote for a candidate by someone who doesn't share your troubles. Local political activists are a potential source of volunteers. Just be careful not to spend too much time courting those who prefer to attend pep rallies than to take part in the day-in-day-out grind of canvassing.

Volunteer recruitment is similar in some ways to fundraising, the other painful campaign task I discussed earlier. You must identify recruits, get them to show up, and track your efforts. That means calling, texting, and/or emailing potential volunteers midweek and slotting them in for canvassing for the upcoming weekend or the following one. It also means asking your family and close friends for help. If you enjoy the luxury of having a volunteer coordinator or campaign manager, train that person to help manage this process because it can become incredibly time-consuming. Because canvassing was important to my strategy, I decided to head up volunteer recruitment and tracking.

Tools of the Trade

Traditionally, you'd provide a canvasser with a folder that would contain a script, a map, a button, and a list of voters organized by name and address plus a clipboard for taking notes and flyers to hand out. The problem is that hard copies slow the process down. Carrying a bag with water, granola bars, and flyers while navigating a paper map and comparing it to a list of persons and addresses is an onerous juggling act, especially when alone.

You're better off using one of the many smartphone apps designed for canvassing efforts. We used Organizer, a simple app that integrates your field map, GPS, and voter data. It also allows you to incorporate a survey of questions to gather from voters. It's much easier to manage than the physical folder system, increasing the number of doors you can hit per hour. It's also incredibly helpful to get a real-time count of how many supporters you've obtained, categorized as Strong Support (SS) or Lean Support (LS). Using an app will also save you the trouble of manually inputting your data later, which is about the last thing in the world anyone want to do after a long day of pounding the pavement. This prevents you from falling behind on data entry and losing the ability to have up-to-date information about your performance, which can help you identify when to shift course.

Any app will have its challenges, though. Ours was glitchy at times. It prompted you to create a new "survey" reach time you added a question. This made it harder to aggregate our data later on down the line since we now had multiple data sets to collate. A word of caution about the number of questions in your survey: at first, I tried to get my canvassers to identify veteran status, pet ownership, and other details. Frankly, most of this information was relatively useless to a campaign as small as ours and actually slowed down our canvassing efforts. Keep your survey to the bare essentials as local races ultimately boil down to a straightforward numbers game.

One of my favorite aspects of using an app was the ability to track individual canvassers' performance over time, including myself. Gauging from my baseline, I could tell when I had a subpar outing and whether I was getting better responses over time. I could also dig into the numbers and see who was having trouble and who were my all-stars. My next-door neighbor Candi, a tall blonde woman, had no difficulty getting people to answer her knocks. She found people home at a whopping rate of 50% while another canvasser who could have played offensive tackle for Whittier College was in the single digits. When I finally realized this, I took our lineman off canvassing duty. I had him do lawn sign deliveries, donation thank-you letters, and other miscellaneous tasks instead. And I actually started paying Candi to hit doors on a more consistent basis. This adjustment paid real dividends as my supporters steadily increased.

Interacting with Voters at the Door

You can't win your campaign at the door, but you can definitely lose it there. Remember, a person's home is where they feel safe and comfortable. You violate this space when you make a poor impression of yourself. If you come across as unprepared, undisciplined, arrogant, rude, sarcastic, or angry, you'll quickly develop a reputation. Word of mouth spreads fast.

Know your issues and have a plan when you knock on someone else's door. Don't expect busy people to do your job for you. It's natural for the person initiating the conversation to carry it at first. Don't start by asking questions, either. (Also, don't refer to voters by name, even though you have this information in your file. It comes off as creepy). Your job at the outset is to quickly introduce yourself and give the voter an idea of why you're running and what you want to accomplish. Listening comes later. Get this information out fast as people are increasingly busy and generally hate solicitors.

If they say, "Sorry, but I'm busy," that can mean "hell no." It can also signify, "I appreciate your effort and will note it when I look over your materials." Or, "I'm shy, and I would prefer to avoid this interaction but thanks." It can also just mean, "I'm busy." Regardless, at least you introduced yourself and showed you're confident and willing to work for votes. If at first you don't succeed, try, try again...on a different occasion.

Honestly, what you say is much less important than how you come across. The so-called 7/38/55 rule tells us that only 7% of communication is verbal.[36] Your voice, on the other hand, conveys 38% of the message. Nonverbal communication (posture, facial expression, gestures, and so on) constitutes most of your communication at 55%, remarkably. So, stand up straight, smile, speak confidently, and look a person in the eyes. It helps to have some talking points (your platform is a good source for this) memorized. You can then riff off them, extemporizing depending on the circumstances, as you focus on coming across positively through your demeanor.

When you're done with your short spiel, go ahead and ask a question. You can only expect to get so far with a one-sided conversation. Hopefully, you took careful note of the voter's house or apartment before you knocked. Ask yourself: What does it say about them? Do they fly an American flag? Do they have a sticker on the window indicating affiliation with a union or support for a particular cause? Is their porch neat and tidy or full of junk? Whatever the case, glean as much as you can from what you see. Combined with the information you have on file, this should give you some idea of which issues will be crucial to the voter. A sixty-eight-year-old white Republican with an American flag and a police union sticker is probably a conservative who values public safety and fiscal prudence. A nineteen-year-old Democrat with a "Coexist" lawn sign and a "Bernie or Bust" bumper sticker is a totally different story. Your task is to be mindful of the differences and find common ground with each (assuming both are people you're targeting for votes). I'm not advocating profiling. What I'm suggesting is that you gather clues to help you find commonalities with your neighbors.

I don't condone you ever getting into a heated argument about politics, national or otherwise, at the door. However, the next part of your discussion must be something of a back-and-forth. Once you find out what the voter cares about, through observation and questioning, try to get the voter to verbalize what they're concerned about in their neighborhood. If they do, you have a golden opportunity. They're offering you the key to their vote. Sometimes just understanding and empathizing will be enough. Other times, helping them understand why their problem exists, even if you can't do anything about it, whether or not you're elected, helps show you're knowledgeable. If their concern is something that you want to change, explain your position and how you can help. This is when the magic happens. When a voter sees you as a viable solution to an urgent problem. (Sometimes, by the way, that problem is a sense of loss of community). When voters see you as a leader who can help unify people, they'll vote for you. They'll see their futures entwined with yours, turning them into loyal supporters.

For example, I knocked on the door of the president of a local neighborhood association. He invited me back for a meet-and-greet. There, I met Robert Arellanes, CEO of a local education nonprofit, LEARN. Robert and I hit it off, and he hosted a meet-and-greet of his own for me. In 2019, Robert invited me to "Rosé All Day," a Fourth of July wine block party on Rose Drive. (This was a fantastic community event until interrupted by the

Ridgecrest Earthquake). I now consider Robert, his significant other Brenda, and his next-door neighbors as friends and supporters – all because, instead of calling it quits for the day, I knocked on one last door.

If you're overly nervous, exhausted, or just stuck, speak to what's written on the handout you give the person at the door when they answer. Doing so helps you remember what to say, and the document also acts as a nice visual aid. It takes the focus off the interpersonal and onto the object for a moment. This allows you to ease into the process of forming a connection with the voter. Now that you've gotten this far, the only thing you have to avoid doing is overstaying your welcome. I usually tried to insert a moment of levity and break it off during a highpoint in our conversation, indicating I was ready to leave by taking a half step toward the street. Make sure you ask for a vote, of course, formalizing support for you. Those who don't ask don't get. Also, make sure the voter knows how to vote for you, whether in-person or by mail. If state law permits you to collect their ballot, offer to do so.

It's okay too if their response to you was tepid, or the voter was figuratively on the fence (literally also). Don't turn someone completely off to you by pestering them. Don't take it personally. It just tells you the voter isn't ready to commit yet or that they like you but will not vote for you and are being nice.

Assume that your opponents will have supporters listening to you. Maybe one in ten residents vocalized support for the opposition in my race even though technically a majority ultimately supported one of my opponents. Never badmouth other candidates even when invited to do so as this might just be a ploy. Assume you're being recorded at all times because you just might be, especially given the prevalence of video monitoring devices. Be mindful not to swear about how your privates feel in the heat while waiting at the door for a resident who it turns out is recording you. That would not be a good look for your campaign. Obviously, don't discuss campaign strategy with anyone either.

When you're done at each door, remember to enter the voter's level of support, or opposition to you, in your smartphone app. Be conservative about evaluating the responses you get. For example, don't take their willingness to listen as leaning toward supporting you unless they've made some overt show of support. You're not doing yourself any favors by inflating your numbers to pump up your ego. Keep in mind that it's normal for you to encounter many undecided voters throughout the race, especially at first.

During the campaign, I covered practically every inch of turf in the district. This helped increase the total number of voters I reached as I didn't ignore any particular area. The other important thing it did was to help me understand the micro terrain. In the Marines, reconnaissance is a vital part of any mission. It helps you avoid the pitfall of making perfect plans in a vacuum, making sure your plan is informed by the facts on the ground.

I learned by canvassing that the community's makeup was radically different from neighborhood to neighborhood and even from street to street. I learned to tailor my sales pitch to what each micro-community tended to care about and to send them volunteers who could relate to them. Much of the difference in perspective among residents stems from the particular safety and quality of life concerns of a given street. One street had its curb painted red halfway up the block and had limited parking. Another had an oil derrick explode some years back, killing one man and burning another badly. One hillside community experienced a rash of burglaries in the days and weeks before I canvassed there. Residents in this area were hesitant to open doors, and the subject came up frequently in our conversations. I decided to leave this area alone for a time and avoided sending canvassers out there late.

There will be times when you come across a disgruntled person. Once, when I knocked on a corner house, a voice thundered, "You put a lawn sign up on my property without permission. It's in the garbage now." I assured him it wasn't me, as I hadn't knocked on his door before. A week later, I noticed my sign was on his lawn. (I'm guessing maybe his significant other felt differently about me). Sometimes people are upset about some federal wedge issue or another and want your opinion on the subject so they can fight with you. Calmly explain that you're running because of your desire to solve local issues. Some will push back, trying to figure out if you're part of their tribe. In my case, they'd try to get me to denounce President Obama or to comment on California's sanctuary cities policy. Rather than get into an argument, just thank them for their time and take your leave. Your goal is to win an election, not to win individual arguments.

Safety Concerns While Canvassing

Depending on whether your election is in the spring or fall, you'll face progressively later sunsets or earlier ones. In my case, with the election in April, the days got longer and longer, giving me extra time for canvassing as the race wore on, particularly when daylight savings started in March. If you're running in November, be mindful that you'll have less time to work with the closer you get to the election and consider front-loading your efforts. Like a marathon runner, build up your miles early on because catching up isn't necessarily possible (since you won't get a good reception bothering people before work or after dark).

Speaking of darkness, make sure you put safety first for you and your volunteers and call it quits early. My friend Daniel had a knife pulled on him during a previous election. In my race, a supporter for one of my opponents made a veiled threat to him about grabbing his shotgun. Avoid staying out too late, don't get too close to the door, and always leave yourself an exit route. Use a buddy system. Use your judgment.

I haven't discussed mailers in detail yet. Suffice to say they'll be an essential part of the campaign. If you see mailers from an opponent, go ahead and take a picture of them. Don't remove any, though, as this is mail theft in violation of federal criminal law. Also, resist the temptation to fiddle in someone's mailbox to avoid the awkward explanation required if someone catches you.

If no one's home, leave a handout at the door but never in a mailbox as this is also a violation of federal law. (That mailbox belongs to the federal government, not the resident, and Uncle Sam charges rent). Keep your composure when six noisy Chihuahuas attack the door after you knock. Lastly, pay attention to any signs prohibiting soliciting or about day sleepers. The first rule of canvassing is to do no harm. I inadvertently failed to heed this to my own detriment. I banged on a door that, no kidding, had a personalized sign saying, "Please do not knock as we have a baby sleeping and large, angry dogs." No sooner had I knocked, and discovered the sign, than two Rottweilers came running up barking loudly with a baby crying in their wake. I felt like the biggest jerk in the world. And you can be sure that I didn't get that particular vote.

One thing I can't prepare you for is the intensity and intimacy of the experiences you will encounter while canvassing. There'll be sublime moments and heartbreaking ones. I'll never forget the satisfaction of ripping into a ripe orange I picked up one sunny weekend afternoon while canvassing in an idyllic hillside neighborhood. Or the kind widow with cancer and a sunny disposition who invited me in for a snack. There was also the time Christina and I were out pounding the pavement. It started raining, us running from door to door without umbrellas, laughing, making conversation with surprised voters while trying unsuccessfully to stay dry.

SUMMARY

- ^ Don't rely on your plan to win it for you. Go out there and compete.
- ^ Don't forget to have fun and get to know your neighbors.
- ^ You and your significant other are your best volunteers.
- ^ Repeat volunteers are better than one-time volunteers.
- ^ Use an app to track your performance.
- ^ Don't argue with voters. Find common ground.
- ^ Assume someone is recording you at all times.
- ^ Stay safe out there.

CHAPTER 15

KILLER CAMPAIGN COMMUNICATIONS

As I mentioned earlier, you can't win an election just by knocking on doors. Owen Newcomer, the Whittier Councilman who lost to Joe Vinatieri in the race for mayor, learned this the hard way when he lost an assembly race in 2006 despite knocking on at least 16,000 doors.[37] Campaigning is a multi-media endeavor. To be competitive, you will want to master the entire suite of campaign messaging techniques, from flyers to phones.

Lawn Sign Wars

There's nothing more self-affirming for a candidate than a street lined with yard signs emblazoned with the candidate's name. Conversely, there's nothing worse than the feeling that an opponent is taking over your turf with each yard sign proof of your inevitable failure. Early on in the race, Irella signs began popping up all over the place., It seemed that she had taken over the district from one day to the next. I called my consultant, Danny. "Man, all this hard work, and she's killing me. You keep saying we're doing great, but how do you know we're not getting shellacked?" Thankfully, Danny, the political veteran, handled the situation with grace. He explained that lawn signs in and of themselves don't do much and how staying the course was ultimately the best thing for the campaign.

Nevertheless, I started a minor yard sign arms race. I bought 500 of them, a seemingly insurmountable number given that I had been giving away just a handful a week. My low acceptance rate made sense to me at the time. After all, politics had become so toxic; why would someone want to risk turning neighbors into enemies?

I came up with a creative way to increase the number of lawn signs I distributed. During the early stages of my campaign, I made too big a show of asking for a lawn sign, saying things like, "It would mean the *world* to me if you would put up a lawn sign." The better approach, I found, is to make it seem like no big deal. Act like taking a lawn sign is part and parcel with supporting a candidate for office, which it is basically. Say something like, "Oh, hey, you don't mind if I put up a small lawn sign here, do you?" You'll get tons of lawn signs up this way.

By making supporters opt-out of a lawn sign rather than opt-in, I increased my number of takers to about eight in ten. The more signs went up, the more people wanted them. By the end of the campaign, people were reaching out to me for them. They wanted one as a badge of honor. All of a sudden, my signs were everywhere.

Unfortunately, my lawn sign troubles weren't over yet. Henderson signs sprung up around the neighborhood like sunflowers from one day to the next. Of course, he had the advantage of a long list of lawn sign takers over the years. He also appeared to be benefiting from local property management companies that would place his lawn signs up in their rental units, sometimes taking mine down. While this practice is inconsiderate of tenants' wishes, it's not unlawful, so I let it go.

Lawn sign fever wasn't limited to Team Henry either. One of Irella's supporters was convinced that I was removing Irella's lawn signs. She sent me text messages pleading, "Can't we all just get along?" Don't be surprised if you, too, get caught up in lawn sign hysteria. Lawn signs are expensive and losing them hurts. When you start to think that the other side might be taking them down as you put them up, it really starts to get your goat up.

The problem is there are plenty of reasons they go away. There are environmental factors like rain or wind. Some residents accept a sign to be polite and then throw them out later (a good reason not to push signs too hard). Others switch candidates. One day while driving, I noticed a big corner house on a major thoroughfare, Beverly Boulevard, had a Henderson sign where mine had once been. This could not be, I thought. It must've been the work of my opponent. After all, I had personally driven to meet this homeowner at the behest of a supporter named Mario, a retired parole officer. I pulled over, whipped out my phone, and texted the homeowner and Mario. The homeowner texted Mario, accidentally leaving me on the exchange, that he was "underwhelmed" by his "boy" (me) and that I had "no vision." Ouch. "Thanks for your consideration. Best of luck in your future endeavors," I wrote, following my better angels. The fact of the matter is that people change their minds. It stings a little, but the day you start getting votes is the day you start losing them.

Campaigning is a lot like law school was for me: long, arduous, and with no validation until the bar exam. The number of lawn signs you put up sometimes feels like getting feedback, like a grade. However, they can be fool's gold. Irella, for example gave out a ton of signs. I came to find out later that her teacher's union volunteers had spent their time knocking on doors and immediately asking to put up a lawn sign and no more. Some voters said yes to be polite. What Irella failed to understand, however, is that the data indicates that lawn signs don't convince people to vote for you. All they do is remind someone who has already committed to voting for you to follow through on election day. By putting lawn signs in the hands of residents who aren't committed to you, or on vacant lots, you're essentially throwing your money away.

This isn't to say distributing lawn signs is fruitless. If you can get a critical mass of them up in your community, it signals to voters that you're the real deal. This tells residents that it's okay to give you their vote because others are too. A flood of lawn signs makes voters feel like they're part of a movement. I had several voters tell me, "Your signs are everywhere!" What these residents were telling me was that our signs indicated to them that we had crossed the threshold from pretender to contender.

Candidate Forums

If you follow national politics, you're probably well acquainted with the debate. At the local level, debates are typically called candidate forums, the difference being that the participants normally don't engage each other directly. The League of Women Voters, the Chamber of Commerce, local unions, and other political groups organize them. In Whittier, there were three such forums. All were filmed, with one, the League's, televised live on local access television. They're as exciting as it gets in terms of local campaign theater, and these events are thus typically standing room only. Because they are public and adversarial, they can inspire nerves like no other facet of a campaign.

What's more, there's no "time off" for these forums. They take place smack-dab in the middle of the election cycle while you're managing fundraising efforts, canvassing, sending mailers, and handling other responsibilities. The temptation will be to wing it, relying on your personality to shine through during the debates. This isn't a plan. This is a form of self-sabotage. Instead, dig down and ready yourself as if you were preparing for a job interview or a big test.

By now, you should know what the issues are in your community. Turn the map around and look at the situation from your questioner's perspective and write down the questions you expect to receive. Better yet, get a group of your closest supporters together and practice answering their questions. And then have them give you feedback on your performance. Make it as realistic as possible. As Norman Schwarzkopf, the general who led Operation Desert Storm, said, "The more you sweat in peace, the less you bleed in war."

By the end of your preparations, you should have written answers to the most likely questions. Distill these answers into a one-page "cheat sheet." Organize them alphabetically by subject matter and put the sheet in a binder you bring up with you on stage. With just a minute or two to answer each question, the difference between a confident, concise answer and a rambling, searching one can be a quick glance at your notes, so make sure they're well organized. If you get a question that you're utterly unprepared for, ask the moderator to repeat the question while you gather your thoughts. Don't prepare long, scripted answers for you to read. It makes you come off as insincere.

I discussed the limits of oral communications in the context of canvassing. It's similar when it comes to candidate forums. Your mastery of the issues isn't an end unto itself but rather a means to convey your confidence, knowledge, maturity, and sincerity. People won't remember your answers so much as how you answered them. What you do when you're not talking matters too. Pay attention and take notes when your opponents are speaking. Avoid making faces, sighing, pouting, smirking, or otherwise acting impetuously. Be courteous with your opponents before and after the forum. It'll show voters you're an adult who can handle the give and take of political life.

At the same time, don't be afraid to be critical of your competition. During the first candidate forum, I was asked how I would continue a tradition of fiscal responsibility on the council. I resented the question because it was biased in favor of the incumbents. I replied by saying that the city no longer merited such a reputation and explained why. Bob scoffed, but too bad. My job was to differentiate myself, not to appease him.

Ultimately, whether your tone is negative or positive matters less than your confidence and authenticity. Voters want leaders who are relatable and human. They've become disillusioned with wishy-washy politicians who aren't what they seem to be. They're looking for a new brand of leader who will both tell and show them who they are so voters can make an informed choice. They're looking for real people, not puppets, to run the show.

Confidence, however, is easily feigned. Two of my opponents were confident to a fault, coming across as overly jocular and clownish. The crowd loved them, which frankly made me a little nervous at first, but laughs don't necessarily equal votes. Authenticity, however, is more challenging to convey, especially in a contrived debate setting. Self-deprecation can help. For instance, I once said, off the cuff, that I had "dad jeans, a dad bod, and dad jokes" at a candidate forum. That comment seemed to connect with the crowd. (One trick to quell nerves is to show up early and greet people in the audience). Ultimately, you must tap into a place of vulnerability and honesty to connect with voters. That takes reconnecting with who you are and why you're running. Just like a Marine rifleman must align rear and front sights to shoot true, your statements about what you believe and what you hope to accomplish must jibe with your genuine reasons for running for you to be relatable.

Finally, I'll offer a few words of advice in no particular order. As I mentioned earlier, good communication works subconsciously. Make sure to have good posture, dress professionally, and to mind your body language. Think of ways to slip your themes into the discussion subtly. I used my tagline "neighbor to neighbor" to emphasize that mine was a grassroots race. Be mindful of the clock but don't hesitate to go over the time limit, even significantly so, if doing so is necessary to make an important point. Don't be obnoxious about it and do it too often, though.

Don't worry if you start slowly in a given candidate forum. My individual performances fell into a come-from-behind pattern. I would read from a prepared opening statement (a crutch, yes, but one I felt I needed at the time). Then I would feel like I had fallen behind compared to the candidates who went completely unscripted and showed more personality. You might feel like folding if you fall behind. When those feelings come, take a deep breath and forge on. Barring a horrible snafu, you can't lose a race during a candidate forum. For you, as an insurgent candidate, the goal is to exceed expectations and distance yourself from the pack. Your primary purpose in a candidate forum is to be taken seriously. That requires showing you can persevere through adversity.

By making a plan, preparing, and fighting through early difficulty, I made it clear that of the four non-incumbents, I was the one serious challenger. That's about the best you can hope for. But even if you do poorly, so long as you have a few good moments, your night is still salvageable. Have someone sit in the front row and record you when it's your turn to speak, or download the full video if the organizer recorded one. Then, take your best moments and put out a highlight reel on your social media page, boosting it to a much larger audience than the one that watched in person. None of the people who missed the event will know you flubbed.

Mailers

Remember all that time I spent talking about fundraising? Here's why. Mailers are the most significant difference between a professional race and one run by amateurs. Anyone can draw up a logo, order some buttons, and knock on a few doors. None of these provide a campaign with the scale necessary to compete in a district election, much less an at-large election.

The strength of mailers lies in how they leverage the power of mass distribution to reach a substantial number of voters and let you simultaneously target just the voters you need to reach using the post office's sorting capabilities. The dilemma you face is that the more people you send a mailer, the cheaper it is on a "per piece" basis but the more expensive overall.

I resolved this dilemma by sending my first mailers to a broader audience, followed by more targeted, progressively cheaper mailers. I sent my first mailer to our entire voter universe. It introduced me and my platform to voters in broad brushstrokes. A biography-focused, introductory mailer is a good idea for anyone new, or even relatively new, to voters. Our next three mailers covered each of the three planks of my platform in turn. Each mailer was sent to an increasingly narrow pool of voters as we crossed people off our list who expressed support for another candidate during canvassing. In this way, knocking on doors saved us hard-earned money.

We then put out two niche mailers. One touted the fact that I was the only candidate endorsed by the Democratic Party. We sent these to Democrat-only households. We also sent a mailer preempting an attack ad. I had learned the importance of "drawing the sting" in the courtroom. I decided to get to the voters first and resolve any concerns before my opponents poisoned the well. We came up with a large bi-fold mailer called "Welcome Home to Whittier," which detailed how I had come to buy a home in Whittier while deployed to Afghanistan and with a baby on the way. It explained how, before my honorable discharge, I'd commuted 300 miles a week, round trip, from Whittier to Twentynine Palms to be with my family in our new home. Be honest with yourself about your weaknesses and closest skeletons. Ask yourself, if I was running against me, how would I hit me? Turn the map around and envision how a negative mailer against you might look. Then figure out how to turn this negativity into a positive for you. Don't just sit there and wait for the blast. If you've made mistakes in your life, find a way to show what you learned from those mistakes. Americans love a turnaround story.

The two niche mailers (the endorsement mailer and the attack ad preemption mailer) we sent were the only ones we hadn't planned from the beginning. They arose out of circumstances we hadn't predicted. When you make your budget, make sure to set aside enough funds for such responsive mailings. The money can come in quite handy if you're forced to defend yourself, or if you decide to go on the attack.

Too many candidates take a "kitchen sink" approach to their mailers. Each mailer has the same message: everything. Not only is this overwhelming for the reader, but the law of diminishing returns dictates that repetitive messages will be increasingly ignored. Make sure your mailers build upon one another. In our case, we sent one mailer introducing me. We then sent three mailers covering each of my respective platform planks. Another mailer delved a little deeper into my personal story, and one last mailer addressed my endorsements. Your goal should be to pique the interests of the voters and keep them interested. That requires having patience and foresight.

It bears mentioning that not all voters receive mailers in the same sequence. For permanent absentee voters, mailers should be spread out over the weeks leading up to the delivery of absentee ballots. On the other hand, poll voters should get the mailers in the days leading up to the election. Since they can only vote on election day, there's no use in getting to them early since you risk having voters forget about you by election day. (Please note that this no longer applies to California, which has moved to a system of universal mail-in ballots).

A million mailers won't make a difference if they aren't any good, of course. There are three aspects to any good mailer. The first is good imagery. My introductory mailer was an excellent example of telling a story with limited text. We used a picture of me with a group of supporters, a picture of me with my family, and a picture of me listening to a voter. Some people read political mailers carefully, but most people, bombarded with junk mail, might only look at your mailer for a split second. You want to convey as much as possible in that time. My introductory mailer wordlessly communicated that I'm a young family man who listens to people and enjoys support from both men and women alike.

Second, good mailers contain quality graphics. Some ideas are difficult to convey in pictures. Accountability was a tough one for us. We used a stock photo of a hand holding a red marker underlining the word "Accountability" in bold. It wasn't a perfect representation, but it was better than dedicating an entire paragraph to the concept. We added a bar graph called "Whittier Safety Trends" that showed how police response times had gone up five minutes since 2013. This put Bob's status as a steady hand when it came to safety into question. A map of my driving route from Twentynine Palms to Whittier in our preemption mailer drove home the point that I'm committed to Whittier, and not some carpetbagger.

Having spent so much time disparaging wordiness, you might find it surprising that the third basic element of a mailer is text. The use of concise, impactful text shows that you know what you're talking about and will be a thoughtful policymaker. I gave specific examples of policies I would pursue to improve accountability in our city and used research to show our ratio of police-to-residents was half the state average. To help liven up my text, we incorporated quotes of me in faux handwriting, conveying a personal touch.

Other best practices include varying the size and shape of mailers. This has the twofold benefit of helping keep the voters' attention and potentially reducing your costs. I sent full-page, half-page, and bi-fold mailers. Using both vertical and horizontal orientations also adds variety to your mail program. Make sure to put your web address and social media handles on all of your materials. Of course, ensure the election date is on the mailer, particularly as it gets close to the big day.

There are some common pitfalls to avoid when it comes to mailers. The first is making sure that you have a disclaimer about who paid for the advertisement. The disclaimer must also include your fundraising committee identification number and the committee's mailing address in California. Missing this can land you in hot water. As can using logos for agencies that haven't endorsed you. Just because you're a member of an organization doesn't mean you have their endorsement. Irella learned this the hard way when she placed the logos of numerous organizations on her website, insinuating official endorsement. Consider using unionized labor for your printing. Failure to have the union imprint, known as the "union bug," will quickly draw the ire of union activists, particularly in a blue state like California.

Finally, I need to cover the elephant in the room: the negative mailer. Regardless of what people say about attack ads, there's a reason they exist: they work. A well-crafted attack ad can be devastating to your opponent. That's not to say there won't be blowback. An attack ad can hurt the sender too. It's, therefore, best to think of negative advertising in relative terms. It's safest to deploy such a tactic in a two-person race. When there are three or more candidates, it becomes highly volatile material. In other words, it can blow up in your face. This is what happened to Bob. When it became clear I wasn't going to attack Irella, his proxies sent mailers labeling her as corrupt and incompetent. This appeared to deflate Irella's numbers (as well as his own) while leaving me relatively unscathed.

The election results indicate that Irella did reasonably well among absentee voters in the more heavily Latino area of Palm Park. Still, her lackluster performance among poll voters there suggests a sharp drop in support for her took place. This tells me the ads against her had their intended effect, causing support for her to dry up as the election grew near. The problem was that Irella's attackers underestimated just how many votes I'd already earned. While the attacks made Bob look harsh and Irella look corrupt, I came across as a reasonable alternative to them both. Eventually, the same proxy who hit Irella, a longtime oilman, sent a lame mailer comparing me to a child, but the effort proved ineffective. They had helped me win the election.

Having done a significant amount of opposition research on both Bob and Irella, I had the option of sending my own negative attack ads. I chose not to for both altruistic and strategic reasons. Strategically, I believed that in attacking Irella, I would be helping Bob argue that I was bringing lowbrow politics to Whittier. I also felt that if I held out long enough, Bob or his allies wouldn't be able to help themselves. And ultimately, they couldn't.

I also held back because something about it didn't feel right. I wanted to win, but I also wanted to win cleanly. I didn't want my boys to be told someday that their father is a dirty politician. I also wanted to be effective once I won, and that meant letting my better angels prevail. Think long and hard about who you want to be as a leader before authorizing an attack ad. It's the point of no return for you as a politician. Make sure you can be proud of yourself when the race is over and also preserve your brand. History shows that losing a bid for office can help you in the long run if your integrity is intact.

With all that said, don't let yourself be mere prey for other, more aggressive politicians. Speak softly but carry a big stick as the adage goes. Do some basic opposition research. There's nothing wrong with knowing what's out there. And suppose you discover misconduct by your opponent that is corroborated by credible evidence. In that case, I'm not even sure that bringing it to light constitutes an attack ad. Just keep in mind that there's no such thing as a response attack ad since it's common practice to hit someone with a negative mailer after it's too late to retaliate.

Social Media

The mere fact of being a young candidate apparently doesn't automatically make you effective at using social media. Four of the eleven candidates in the April 2018 Whittier election were millennials. Still, only one managed to win, me. The others had a social media presence and posted regularly but never managed to gain significant followership. Meanwhile, I was able to increase my followers from zero to about 1,200 in six months. That might not sound like a lot when Kylie Jenner has over 20 million Facebook followers. However, in local races, where the margin of victory can be in the single digits, cultivating hundreds of online supporters and communicating with them in an instant can be incredibly powerful.

Social media, however, is an afterthought for most politicians. Me on the other hand, I treated it like a job. Because I had so many disadvantages going into my race, I looked at social media as one of the few areas where I was clearly superior to my opponents. So,

I committed myself to squeezing all I could get out of the thing. Knowing early on that it would play an essential part in my campaign, I budgeted a substantial amount in paid promotions. I stretched myself during fundraising to ensure I would have a full $6,000 social media budget. I doubt any of the eleven other candidates that cycle spent even $500.

Once I had the money, the question became how exactly to spend it for maximum effect. Twitter is known for its partisanship and acerbic content. This wasn't in line with my desired strategy or image, so I skipped the platform altogether. Instagram is more focused on images than text and thus limits what you can say. It's better for selfies and food shots than political campaigns. Facebook, on the other hand, has a relatively older demographic, and political content has become commonplace there. Many community groups practically live on Facebook, so it became a natural place to focus my attention.

The first step is to create a public figure profile. Some candidates prefer to use their private accounts rather than go through this trouble. I understand the temptation as starting a new profile seems foolish when you already have a following of sorts among your existing Facebook friends. Still, this is a big mistake. Not creating a public profile limits your ability to reach new users, referred to on Facebook as "reach." On Facebook, there are two types of reach, organic and paid. Organic reach refers to those users who see your posts because they've liked your page (or because people who've liked your page have shared it, or your posts, with their own friends). People outside your network of followers see posts you boosted because you've paid to "reach" them.

Regardless of whether you pay to message potential followers or not, content is ultimately king when it comes to Facebook. It takes a lot more money to spread boring content far and wide than exciting content. I found this out the hard way by relying primarily on a boilerplate ongoing paid promotion. I put maybe $10 behind it per day as a test run. It carried a photograph of my family and me with a line that said something like, "I'm running for Whittier City Council because I believe in transparency, safety, and prosperity." Exactly. Boring. The non-paid posts I was making at the time primarily consisted of me attending events. The problem was no one really cared if I went to the Chamber of Commerce's Wake Up Whittier networking mixer.

Posts about events that you throw are impactful, on the other hand. As I mention in the following section on meet-and-greets, conveying the idea that your events are well attended and popular is a powerful, validating message. It says, "It's okay to vote for me. Others are too." So, let people know when you're doing well. Let them know when a family invites you in during a backyard barbecue while canvassing, or when you reach a milestone in terms of the number of Facebook followers you have.

To captivate an audience's attention with a post, you need three elements. First, the subject matter needs to be timely. You need to convey a sense of urgency on the issue. "My name is so and so and I'm running for office" fails that criterion. You have to highlight what's at risk if you lose. If you're running against an incumbent, that means more of the status quo, more of the same. Explain what the status quo is and what the result would be if it were maintained. Make sure people know that a vote for you isn't just change for change's sake but rather change for the sake of a better alternative.

Second, the post has to be packaged effectively. That means images are superior to mere text, and videos are better than images. And any text must convey the subject powerfully and succinctly—no long dissertations. People simply don't feel they have the time to read long posts. Remember, you're competing with an entire Internet of cat videos and ice bucket challenges. This is where shelling out a few bucks for a designer to create graphics to go along with your posts pays off.

Lastly, your post should ideally be thought-provoking in some way, emphasis on the "thought" part. Merely provoking people isn't enough. Anyone can be a provocateur. Because of where we are as a culture, shocking sells. You can peddle conspiracy theories, unverified accusations, and other nastiness, and it might get some traction. Yet it's not going to get you what you're after – votes. My guess is those people who are quick to criticize online tend to lack the follow-through and commitment to voice their displeasure at the ballot box. This is especially true of local, down-ballot races – their righteous indignation is satisfied when they hit like or leave a nasty comment.

My best example of a thought provoking post was when I posted about Uptown, which I felt it had fallen into disrepair, I believed, in part because Bob wanted to keep it a sleepy backwater. So, I obtained twenty-one high-resolution pictures of various locations that were in decay (graffiti, cracking sidewalks, grime, vomit) and posted them. I included a caption that read, "If a picture is worth a thousand words, here are 21,000 words on how our city has willfully ignored Uptown Whittier." I pointed out that instead of fixing the streetscape, the city was going to spend the vast majority of its Uptown capital funds on a large parking structure. The post took off immediately. I boosted it with maybe $200 and watched as about 20,000 people saw my post, and a significant online discussion took hold. It was incredible. I even started having residents parroting their disdain for the parking structure back to me at the door! I had created a new campaign issue with the click of a button.

From then on, I was a truthsayer for many voters. Bob primarily communicated with the public through city council meetings, which relatively few people watched, and at a smattering of public events, which relatively few people attended. I figured people in West Whittier would appreciate being told directly what was going on in their community. I found the politics and history of Whittier fascinating, so I just started to explain. I did it through blog posts, by making videos on various subjects – parks, Uptown, transportation. Showing that you understand the issues and can explain them creates a sense that you can be entrusted with running a city.

For many candidates, social media is what they do until the election gets too busy, and then it falls off. It needs to be the opposite for you to truly succeed at using social media to its fullest potential. Social media is at its most compelling when it's used to document your lived experience for followers. (I learned this while documenting my preparations for an amateur boxing tournament while stationed in Twentynine Palms).[38] You want voters to feel like they're along for the ride with you. Keep your eyes peeled every day for opportunities to involve your audience in what you're doing. For example, the day I dropped my mail-in ballot off at the post office, I had Christina film me placing it into the receptacle. As I did this, I spontaneously smacked the top of the bin, chuckling. It was short, almost GIF-length. That video reached 12,302 people – without boosting. It's always better to show rather than tell people what you want them to know. Instead of telling them about oil drilling in the community, I went and found an active well in a residential neighborhood and filmed it in action – reaching 8,877 people.

Whether it's because people are too busy or because they have an aversion to politics, voter participation can be dismal in local races. Use social media to remove as many obstacles as you can for people to vote. Tell people when and where to vote both at the polls and by mail. I commissioned a simplified, scaled-down map of voter precincts. I posted it to Facebook, along with multiple reminders to vote. I recently read a study that showed some young people don't vote because they claim they don't know where to buy stamps.[39] Instead of poking fun at their ignorance, show people how to turn in a mailer. Be creative. Make voting meaningful and fun.

Find ways to show voters you're working hard to earn their votes. I did this by using posts of me doing things like participating in neighborhood cleanups and other events. One incredibly successful post included a picture of a worn pair of my Converse low tops. Near the election date, I also posted a photo slideshow paired with the song "Everyday" by Logic with the refrain, "I work hard every day." The message was clear: I won't take you for granted.

Follow your performance closely and make sure you get a sense of what posts are working better than others. Your ability to spread your message on Facebook depends on getting people to interact with your posts. This is known as "engagement." That's because you can invite people who like your posts to like your page, and once they like your page, they'll receive your posts free of charge. The more comments and shares you get, the more widely your posts are disseminated. Add trending hashtags and tag various groups on posts relevant to them to reach an even wider audience. Post to local pages with potential voters under your candidate profile.

Don't forget, though, that what you're ultimately doing through social media is telling a story, filling in a void left behind by reduced local news coverage. You're not just selling your ideas or personality. You're offering a chance for residents to be part of something bigger than themselves, a community. You're a vehicle for increased civic engagement. You bolster civic participation when residents become invested in your story, your efforts, and your campaign. One of the best compliments someone can pay me is to tell me how they feel part of the political process thanks to my social media efforts.

Meet-and-Greets

In a sense, meet-and-greets are the in-person progression of what happens on social media. Social media creates the feeling that you're getting to know a candidate and what they're about without meeting that person. A meet-and-greet is when you actually meet the candidate in real life and get to know the person behind the image. For those of you who aren't great with large crowds, the meet-and-greet is a wonderful opportunity to operate in a more comfortable, small-group setting.

Setting up a meet-and-greet is relatively easy. A local coffee shop or bookstore will do just fine. Make sure you incorporate at least one meet-and-greet a month into your budget so that you can have food and drinks covered. I typically handed the coffee shop my campaign debit card and instructed attendees to give my name at the register. You can also use a voucher system if your event is in a crowded place. You can get as creative as you want when siting the meet-and-greet. I kept it basic out of necessity, given the volume of my campaign activity, using coffee shops as my go-to destination.

You might want to consider branding your meet-and-greets. I called mine "Hump Day with Henry" and scheduled them for the first Wednesday of each month. Keeping a regular date made the event easier to remember, as did the catchy name. I held them at a different coffee shop each time, promoting the events on Facebook. All but one was well attended. I also hosted a meet-and-greet at a deli on a Saturday during lunch, to make myself available to people who were busy Wednesday evenings. This event had a particularly good turnout, perhaps a dozen people or more. When that happens, you and your campaign get a tremendous shot in the arm. Such meet-and-greets are also great photo ops too. Meet-and-greets aren't just a way to get exposure and public validation. They're also a way for you to learn more about how local issues affect people in the community and verify how your message is coming across. Whereas there's no back-and-forth at a candidate forum and residents usually just want you off their porch as fast as possible during canvassing, at a meet-and-greet, the people there want to engage with you. That means you should be refining your platform as you hear what residents say when they're comfortable enough to speak candidly with you.

The worst part of hosting a meet-and-greet is sitting there, wondering whether anyone will show up. On one occasion, a cold and dreary day, no one actually showed up to my event. Make sure to invite your closest supporters to these events. The last thing you want is to be seen at a public gathering place hosting an event by yourself. Also, try to host meet-and-greets after you're done canvassing. Otherwise, your canvassing efforts will suffer. I held my hump days in the evening after canvassing was called for the day.

In addition to public meet-and-greets, I would urge you to hold as many private meet-and-greets as possible. These are different in that they're held at private homes. Usually, the host, one of your supporters, is responsible for bringing guests and providing refreshments. The more success you experience, the greater the chances people will ask to host one for you. Such events are fantastic because they bring out people who might not have otherwise been inclined to support you had it not been for the fact that their neighbor hosted the event. I tended to hold these on weekend evenings. If the host is a strong supporter, you can expect wine, backslapping, and a few donations, which are always helpful and appreciated.

My most memorable meet-and-greet was thrown by a local photographer who reached out to me on Facebook Messenger, asking me how I felt about LGBTQ rights. After reading my response, he offered to throw me a meet-and-greet with members of Whittier's gay community. The event was incredibly fun, required little to no preparation on my part, and paved the way for the first-ever Whittier Pride festival, which I helped organize in 2019.

Interviews

While the impact of giving interviews to local periodicals, college newspapers, Facebook groups, or community news blogs is unclear, I would urge you to do them anyway. The printed interview is a suitable format for explaining your platform and background. (Podcasts are a growing medium too). Niche publications, digital or otherwise, also help you get out in front of an audience that might not have otherwise been available to you. For example, I didn't knock on student doors at the local liberal arts school, Whittier College, out of respect for student privacy. Instead, I interviewed with their Quaker Campus newspaper.[40] This helped get my name out to students and even led to an endorsement by this newspaper (speaking at their student senate meeting helped too).

When you participate in an interview, keep in mind that the interviewer will pick and choose what they publish and that only the most attention-grabbing information will see the light of day. As you formulate your answers, try to package what you say into concise, clean sound bites that are likely to grab the consumer's attention. Your goal should be for your words to make up the headline, as many people sadly don't read past it nowadays.

Indicators of Success

Running for office is an adaptive, iterative process. What I mean by this is that it continually changes, taking on a life of its own. You must learn and adapt to succeed. When people ask me what it's like to run for office, I liken it to a snake or an insect shedding its exoskeleton and putting on a new one. It's an arduous process during which you undergo a metamorphosis. If you're the same person coming out that you were going in, you surely didn't take it seriously enough.

I personally changed quite a bit. Being a politician moderated some of my worst impulses. Ironically, I became less, not more, prideful. I also became less reactive, more willing to let a personal slight or offense slide, and more patient. Required to interact with people from all backgrounds, I was forced to find common ground with a broader audience. I was no longer the person seeking escapism and validation through careerism. I was now a devoted community advocate.

Aside from your subjective personal growth, there are precious few indicators of success at your disposal. As I mentioned earlier, campaigning is similar to law school – the results come at the end. That doesn't mean there aren't *any* signs. Your best indicators of success are your personal performance metrics. This is where using an app while canvassing pays off. A strong indication that you're doing well is that your conversion rate at the door, the ratio of your supporters to that of your opponents, steadily improves. As the election draws near, you should find less and less undecided voters and more voters committing to a side. The key is to make sure you're doing better than your opponents. Remember, you don't need to win all the votes, just a majority (or a plurality in races involving multiple candidates).

Another good sign is that you're on pace to reach your win number. Don't emulate what some candidates do and try to pull the race out at the last minute like some college student cramming for a final exam. As I'll explain in the following chapter, the final week is basically a wash for you when it comes to canvassing. Making sure you hit your magic number when it counts is a matter of keeping an eye on the numbers from week to week.

Perhaps the best indicator comes during the week or two before the election when the names of voters who have submitted absentee ballots start rolling into the election official or city clerk.

Your consultant should cross-reference this list with your pledged supporters to get an idea of how many of your absentee voters have mailed in their ballots. While you don't have access to how they voted for privacy reasons, the more of your committed voters who voted by mail, the better you're doing. Finally, word of mouth, the least reliable source of information, plays a role in a local election. Pay attention to what people are saying about you and about your opponents. If people aren't talking about you, then you probably aren't doing too well. In Whittier, we're lucky to have a thriving political culture, so finding the scuttlebutt isn't all that hard. If your local political culture is not quite as robust, that just means you have to work harder to find out who the bellwethers are and what they're saying about your race. You might start by sticking around after a candidate forum and asking what people thought of your performance. With that said, don't overreact to negative feedback about you. Sometimes it's actually the best sign that you're a real challenger.

SUMMARY

^ Don't stress out over lawn signs. Give them out if you can, but don't worry if they're lost or stolen. They don't really bring in votes.

^ Candidate forums are nerve-wracking but don't lose your cool. You can recover from a stumble.

^ Prepare for a candidate forum like a job interview because, in a way, it is one.

^ Learn to disagree without being disagreeable.

^ Make sure to film your debate performances for your highlight reel.

^ Mailers are costly but they scale up well.

^ Use mailers to preempt attack ads on you.

^ Vary the shape and size of your mailers and minimize the use of text.

^ Don't forget to put a disclaimer on your mailers indicating its source.

^ Think hard before using a negative mailer as it could backfire.

^ Social media is increasingly powerful but has its limits.

^ Make sure your posts are timely, urgent, visual, and thought-provoking.

^ The best social media is participatory and builds community.

^ Meet-and-greets are great photo and learning ops.

^ Create your own feedback loop by collecting data on your canvassing performance and reviewing it consistently.

RESOURCES

For examples of lawn signs, a sample candidate forum cheat sheet, videos of my candidate forum performances, and PDFs of my mailers, please visit authorhenrybouchot.com.

CHAPTER 16

GOTV: GETTING TO THE FINISH LINE

You might think that the week leading up to the election is just like the previous weeks. You would be wrong. The focus is entirely different. In the weeks leading up to the last week of the race, the goal is to court enough supporters to win the race. The final week leading up to the election, on the other hand, is about getting your voters to come out to the polls and vote, or to drop off their mail-in ballots, whatever the case may be. That's what they mean by "getting out the vote." This requires a certain amount of foresight and self-control. Your game plan must account for a few days where you're no longer knocking on doors and asking for votes. That means you have to get to your win number a week early.

My mantra the week of the election – the one that kept me sane – was: "The race has already been won or lost." Sounds depressing, but it's a lot better than, "I will make up for what I failed to do earlier now." After coming up short by just a few dozen votes in her race, Lizette's supporters complained of discrepancies on the ballot, what some dubbed the "bubble trouble."[41] They held a press conference decrying the injustice of having a blank write-in candidate bubble so close to the named candidates (despite some evidence that the words "Write-In Candidate Here" can actually confuse voters).[42]

Going all-in means holding yourself accountable and not making excuses. It means getting the votes you need before Get Out the

Vote (GOTV) week. Most people lose on the first try. With this book in hand, your chances will be better, but you might still lose. If that happens to you, maintain your dignity and live to fight another day. Be a winner, not a whiner. Respect the democratic system and remember that the election is about more than just your coronation. Above all, focus your time on getting your vote out, not playing catch up, deploying gimmicks, or pointing fingers.

"Alright, alright," you say. So, if I'm not supposed to try for new votes during the final week, what *am* I supposed to do? Good question. Your strategy should now shift to systematically and efficaciously reminding all of your pledged voters to actually vote. This is where the app you used to track your supporters during the many weeks of canvassing pays off.

Start out by you getting a list of every poll voter who's indicated they'll support you from your consultant and exporting these names and addresses onto stickers. Print extra copies of one of your mailers or, if you have extra money, hire a graphic designer to create a flyer with a hole big enough for a doorknob. (Remember, this is for poll voters only. Your absentee voting supporters will vote by mail). Get your volunteers to drop these reminders off at the corresponding addresses. There is no need to stop and chat. Just leave them at the door. The goal is to remove the excuse of, "I didn't know where to go." You are also giving a subtle reminder: "Hey, remember you promised to vote for me? Well, the day is here," or practically here. This is a time-consuming activity. (You'll appreciate your mail carrier after this). Allot yourself the weekend (Saturday and Sunday) before the Tuesday election to carry this out.

If you've been paying close attention, you might've noticed that I've yet to mention phone banking as a means of getting votes.

That's because it's a relatively ineffective way of convincing people to vote for someone as it lacks the essential face-to-face interaction involved in door-to-door canvassing. However, in the week leading up to the election, it's an excellent tool for getting out the vote. Set yourself up with phone banking software that'll call up numbers from your list of supporters, connecting you when a live person is ready. The software should be programmed so that you can leave a prerecorded voicemail. Your message should remind the recipient to vote and when and where. Your political consultant should be able to give you a recommendation for what software to use and how to avoid violating any telecom regulations.

You might also want to consider putting together a robocall. Admittedly, these calls are annoying. The voter picks up the phone and a voice recording begins, offending their ears. You have to consider the cost-benefit of alienating voters this way. Still, there are times when a robocall is a good idea. For instance, I noticed that I did great with native Spanish speakers at the door. However, the difficulty in reaching people at home during canvassing made getting to these voters efficiently a challenge. I was at risk of losing votes simply because I lacked a Spanish surname (almost 40% of Whittier's population speaks a language other than English at home, per the U.S. Census Bureau). So, I recorded a robocall in Spanish and sent it to native speakers. Use your discretion, of course, but I would err on the side of hitting send on a robocall even if it annoys some people. Just because they're a little annoyed with you doesn't mean you won't get their vote.

In addition to reminders at the door and robocalls, I carpeted the electorate toward the end with newspaper advertising, lawn signs, and a spike in social media spending. This is the incapacitating crescendo I described during my earlier strategy discussion. While the decline of local newspapers is well documented and real, those who continue to subscribe are often high propensity voters. The problem is that print ads are expensive. Getting a full-page spread can quickly devastate your budget, and its effectiveness is questionable. If all you want is to remind people to vote for you, something less than a large print ad will do. For me, that meant a sticker on the front page of the newspaper on Saturday (our early voting day) and on election Tuesday. These were simple (just my logo and the election date) and cheap. For a little over a thousand bucks, I was able to get stickers on thousands of printed newspapers plus banner ads on the *Whittier Daily News* website.

This is about as creative as I got when it came to GOTV. Vincent McLeod, by contrast, decked a bicycle out with his lawn signs and a boom box and rode around town promoting his campaign. It's not really in my personality to clown around like that. More importantly, his effort wasn't targeted at likely voters and thus had limited benefit.

I did, however, put lawn signs up on street corners throughout the city the night before the election. I realize that I mentioned before that lawn signs aren't for getting out votes, that they're for reminding lawn sign takers of the social contract they made to vote for you. This, however, was about "shock and awe."

You'll need to get a posse of your friends to do this in the evening before the race for maximum effect. (You also might need to purchase extra lawn signs if you've run out). Put the lawn signs out in teams of two for safety reasons. And make sure your volunteers don't put them in medians or the right of way (again, for obvious safety reasons). It's a good feeling to wake up and see that your lawn signs have sprung up throughout the city or district.

On election day, you're going to be a very busy person. And because of your lawn sign adventures the night before, you're going to be pretty wiped. You've got to suck it up and push through. If you've put in the work, you should enjoy a comfortable lead, and the last day likely won't make the difference. Your efforts on election day are basically for your peace of mind. I've met quite a few people with tales of woe about how they ran for office and lost by a small number of votes. In some cases, decades have passed, and the memory is still bitter for them. Run through the finish line so you don't have to live with a close loss hanging over your head, forever wondering what might have been.

On the day of the election, your political consultant should give you an alphabetical list of your supporters organized by precinct. Allocate two volunteers per precinct to monitor the polls for you. These need to be your best, most reliable volunteers. They'll be just outside of where voting is taking place. They have three jobs to do.

The first is to watch for irregularities. Poll workers – the seasonal employees who get paid to handle the voting – aren't permanent staffers and sometimes make mistakes. Make sure you and your volunteers know the election rules because the poll workers sometimes won't. For example, an absentee voter can show up and drop off their ballot in person. If the absentee voter has lost their ballot, they can vote in person. If an absentee voter shows up with their mail-in ballot, they can surrender it and vote at the poll. A precinct voter can vote at any precinct. Of course, these were the California rules as of 2018, and you should be mindful of your own state's current regulations. The point is that you and your volunteers need to keep an eye out to keep poll workers from unintentionally detering people from voting by giving out the wrong information.

The second poll monitor task is to cross supporters off the list as they come in. You're not to ask voters who they are, how they voted, or interact with them in any way other than maybe acknowledging a hello or a smile. In fact, your poll monitors shouldn't even wear campaign paraphernalia. Otherwise, you're at risk of electioneering, which is the improper influencing of voters at polling places. Charges of electioneering can potentially cloud your victory. Poll workers will maintain their own list of who's come in to vote. They'll update this list at periodic intervals per local election law. You're allowed to inspect their list – they keep more than one copy for this very reason – but they'll also keep an updated list on the polling location door. Your volunteers will need to reconcile this list with your own, crossing your supporters off as they arrive. This allows you to provide your other volunteers with an up-to-the-minute call list for reminding supporters to come in and cast a ballot.

Of course, you want to have the most up-to-date information, but keep in mind that polling precincts aren't the CNN Situation Room. They're low-tech operations managed by poorly paid people. Be kind to the poll workers. This pays off in the last hours of the campaign, as voters coming home from work pile up at the door, and updates become less predictable.

Armed with your list, you'll need a small army of volunteers to call, call, call. Tread carefully when text messaging voters.

Make sure not to use a completely automated system. Call and leave a voicemail, then wait a reasonable amount of time before calling again. You run the risk of annoying voters, but this is their civic duty after all and they did make a promise to you, so don't feel too guilty asking them to hold up their end of the bargain. If they do answer and say that they're unable to get to the polls because of a disability or lack of transportation, offer to pick them up if you have enough volunteers hanging around. If they vote by mail, offer to pick up and drop off their absentee ballot. It's perfectly legal, at least in California.

Your poll monitors' third and final task is to look out for improper behavior by your opponents or others. Electioneering runs counter to a free and fair election system. You should report inappropriate behavior to your election official. In my race, for example, I observed a supporter for one of my opponents handing out flyers in the polling location's vicinity and trying to sneak her voters to the front of the line. As much as I hated to get involved, I pointed her out to poll workers, and they made her stop. Also be on the lookout for any improper behavior by city workers. Whether by incompetence or incumbency bias, it's not unheard of to hear of local police undertaking traffic enforcement around a precinct or notice construction projects spring up near a polling location. If this happens, reach out to the city attorney and clarify that such activity is illegal and unacceptable.

Where exactly should you be as the candidate? You should be at what the Marines call the "point of friction." This is where the action is happening, where you have the best chance of influencing the race. This will typically be your busiest polling precinct, the one with the most voters, the worst parking, the heaviest traffic, and the most stressed-out poll workers. Park yourself outside and supervise your volunteers. Take the time to call supporters who you haven't crossed off your master list yet. Don't get so sucked into your phone, though, that you're not watching to make sure volunteers are making calls or to recruit more volunteers.

Based on the number of people on my list of supporters who failed to show up to vote on the day of the election, I figured we were toast. And yet I pulled it off. Voter no-shows were seemingly bolstered by others who we'd never engaged one-on-one at the door. This reinforced my belief in the importance of a diversified communications strategy. I was relieved because I was so exhausted at this point that I couldn't imagine coming back for a second run.

The last thing left to do is to go to your election night party. Make sure you allocate a few hundred bucks in your budget and get enough food and drink for your supporters, family, and friends who'll want to share the moment with you. Especially if you win, you'll need a fair amount of, ahem, refreshments on hand as additional people will waltz in to congratulate you. If possible, organize the event at a restaurant or a bar, or at someone else's house. The last thing you want to do is clean up after a long night of celebrating. If you're really paranoid, you can go monitor the count. (The County of Los Angeles has since taken over our elections, making for a lot less drama as votes take weeks to completely tally).[43] The vote count was on local access cable for us and conducted by a neutral third party consultant so I skipped it in favor of being at my party. I'm glad I did because the experience was quite the thrill with Bob leading all the way until the final precinct.

SUMMARY

^ GOTV is about reminding supporters to vote, not finding new supporters.

^ Increase your spending in the final week of the election. Use door hangers, phone banking, robocalls, social media ads, and newspaper ads to remind your supporters to vote.

^ Election day will be busy, but it's rarely determinative.

RESOURCES

For a day-by-day GOTV timeline, examples of door hanger mailers, a list of phone banking and robocall software, and pictures from my election night, please visit authorhenrybouchot.com.

PART IV

POST ELECTION

"No man undertakes a trade he has not learned, even the meanest; yet everyone thinks himself sufficiently qualified for the hardest of all trades, that of government."

– **SOCRATES**

THE GOLDEN OPPORTUNITY

The snapshot of my Moment of Triumph
Is adorned by a volunteer's happy crack
His jeans as low as his joy is high
Hands reaching toward the sky
Down six votes with one precinct left
As the final tally is announced
Henderson 141, Bouchot 246
The takedown now dealt
The absurdity of the moment captured by the volunteer's butt
And me my face buried in my hands
Seemingly overcome
The fearsome reality sinking in
The golden opportunity is won

CHAPTER 17

BE CAREFUL WHAT YOU WISH FOR

Poor Christina. She had taken almost a month off from work to support my campaign – two weeks to canvass leading up to the election and two weeks after it to vacation. Now, she found me immersed in the world of local government rather than taking a break. Instead of relaxing, I was reading budgets and meeting with staff on a range of issues: historic preservation, parks, funding, infrastructure, economic and real estate development, even Robert's Rules of Order. It was like sucking water through a fire hose. With the budget season in full swing and a looming pension crisis, easing into my new role didn't seem like an option. To complicate matters, I was replacing a living legend in Bob Henderson.

People are paying the most attention to you when you start a new position, which also happens to be when you're least prepared. It would be incumbent upon me to hit the ground running, especially given who I was taking over for. So, I went above and beyond. I visited city parks with staff, met with constituents about a pending hillside development, and attended local events like Earth Day. I set up meetings with groups I would need to work with, like the Whittier Uptown Association and the Whittier Conservancy. There were also ethics forms to complete, a portrait to take, and lots of congratulatory phone calls to take.

I hadn't given much thought during the election about what might happen if I won since it seemed like a luxury I could deal with if it actually happened. There was also a superstitious aspect to my denial – I didn't want to jinx myself by taking a win for granted. To be honest, I also didn't want to increase my disappointment if I lost. You'll be tempted to take the same ostrich approach, but I urge you to start thinking about what you'll do if you win. Be careful what you wish for, as the saying goes, since it just might come true. Armed with the lessons in this book, you'll have a good chance of achieving your dream of holding elected office.

A People Business

I could certainly have been in worse shape. I had experience working in government. I knew the basics of how a council-manager form of government works. The City Manager is the executive responsible for managing the entire staff, including the police chief. The city manager is also responsible for implementing the will of the council. Meanwhile, the city council is responsible for setting the city's policies and objectives and approving its annual budget, with its staff, city attorney, and civilian commissioners' advice. However, I didn't have a plan for what I would do on day one. I hadn't even started, and I was already behind.

Complicating matters, each of my new colleagues, including Josue, had come out in support of my opponent. I was within my rights to come out of my corner swinging. At the same time, I wanted to avoid behaving in a manner that would bring shame to other young minorities seeking office. I also had an ambitious policy agenda and would need help from my colleagues. I made sure to express my eagerness to collaborate with them during interviews and praised Bob and his contributions to the city.[44] Over the next couple of weeks, I met for lunch with each of my new colleagues, setting the stage for a collegial relationship.

Put aside the assumptions you have of your fellow elected officials and get to know them as people. Ultimately, no one else in the city knows what you're experiencing like they do. Even if they're diametrically opposed to you in terms of political philosophy, search for common ground and, critically, assume they're in it for the right reasons until proven otherwise.

They say politics is a relationship business and this is undoubtedly true. What you might not expect is just how many types of relationships are involved. To be at your best, you must mind these different types of relationships and tend them in a way that maximizes your effectiveness. I can't overemphasize how critical having a positive relationship with your City Manager is to your success. Cities get themselves into scandals and budgetary problems when relationships among its key players become dysfunctional. If you belittle the City Manager, the city's chief executive, or if staff sees you as an impetuous tyrant, you'll be swimming against the tide. Worse, you might be sabotaged.

With that said, don't tolerate maltreatment either – your office demands respect. For instance, we recently fired a consultant who told me to shut the you-know-what-up during a virtual council meeting, accidentally leaving his microphone on.[45] It's okay to be friendly with staff – you don't need to act like a robot. But above all, be professional. If staff members feel you respect and appreciate their efforts, they'll work hard to ensure you're successful. That doesn't mean you can't criticize them on occasion. You need to have the courage to call staff out when they do shoddy work. And sometimes, this is simply a matter of unavoidable political theater. However, the general leadership principle still stands that you should criticize in private and praise in public.

Make a Game Plan

With my colleagues and staff covered, I moved on to creating a game plan. You might be thinking, well, why not just pursue my platform? A platform is what you would attain all things being equal. However, not all matters are ripe all at once. It takes patience, diligence, and, most of all, good timing to advance your agenda.

Given that I'd only won a plurality of the vote, I decided to take a measured, inclusive approach. The fact of the matter was that most voters in my district hadn't voted for me. I needed to make sure I would be seen as a councilman for all voters, not just those who voted for me. That meant patience on items like the parking structure, which I'd vehemently opposed during the race.

Considering the political realities, I decided to support the parking structure and push for one-time investments in my district instead. This approach proved surprisingly successful, possibly because it came as a relief to my colleagues who may have been bracing for the worst from me. I had little trouble securing immediate improvements for my district, such as a protective barrier around the Central Park playground and a lighted crosswalk across the street, new playground equipment at Broadway Park, and new fitness equipment at Guirado Park.[46]

My success wasn't limited to park improvements, though. I started several critical initiatives with my colleagues' help, including a potential bus route extension through my district. I received several important committee assignments, including the Metro Gold Line Extension Subcommittee, a massive project that could redefine our town. Not everything was roses and rainbows, of course. I met resistance when it came to replacing Bob as our representative to the Puente Hills Habitat Authority.[47] However, by focusing on relatively noncontroversial local improvements and by being a decent colleague, I was effective from the get-go.

Small victories are acceptable at the outset while you're getting your sea legs under you. Eventually, though, you'll want to select a few big-ticket items you're passionate about and wish to pursue. This is what I refer to as playing "the long game." It's what will help brace you for the slings and arrows that'll be aimed your way (don't read your hate mail as they say) and keep you motivated and shuffling forward. Playing the long game will help you determine when you need to put up a fight, when to hold them and when to fold them, taking a strategic loss. For me, the three critical issues for the next four years were addressing homelessness,[48] revitalizing Uptown,[49] and bringing the Gold Line to Whittier.[50] If I could accomplish these three goals, I would consider my term a resounding success. (Spoiler alert: I did).

Sometimes, though, your most significant accomplishments come unexpectedly. Make sure you're open to changing your plan. This happened when I teamed up with local LGBTQ community members to create the first Pride festival in Whittier's history. This wasn't something I'd had in my mind during my campaign, but when I saw how important such an event would be for the community, I jumped in both feet first. And the results were astonishing. Thousands showed up to celebrate. People who had felt shunned for years now said to me, "I never expected to see something as amazing as this in Whittier!"[51]

So, What's It Like?

A common question I get when people learn I'm a politician is, "What's it like?" It reminds me of the difficulty of answering what it's like to go to war in that the answer isn't exactly pretty. Like war, being a local elected official is a complex mixture of the strange, the exciting, and the mundane.

First off, it can be lonely sometimes. People start treating you differently, for one, sometimes way too nicely and other times, well, not so much. Your supporters stop calling you because they worry that you're too busy, and sometimes you are. Your opponents, meanwhile, clamor for your attention. This can make you want to retreat into yourself. You'll also invariably be criticized, sometimes harshly. People who supported you but only because you supported their particular issue during the campaign will want to crucify you for changing your mind. This happened to me when Rick the photographer disavowed me for not opposing the Uptown parking structure. Be patient with your supporters and opponents and remind yourself, and them, that keeping an open mind is a virtue, despite what our prevailing political culture tells us. Acknowledge that change is difficult for everyone and work to convince your supporters of your evolving vision.

Second, you'll need to adjust to being somewhat famous. I say "somewhat" because unlike an actual celebrity who can't go anywhere without being noticed, most people in your city won't recognize you. You'll walk into a room where you're the honored guest only to get treated rudely at some local establishment like any other Joe Schmo afterward. It's like when Superman goes back into the phone booth and reverts to Clark Kent. It's nice in a way because you retain a semblance of privacy. What makes serving in local government different, however, is that your neighbors are also your constituents. There's no governor's mansion or White House to retreat to when you're eventually mired in a controversial issue. The fact that it's your neighbors, and the occasional fellow churchgoer, attacking you can make holding local office uncomfortable and isolating.

It takes time, but you'll eventually feel like your usual self, perhaps too much so. You might feel the urge to flip off that motorist who cut you off or get snarky with the gas station attendant who was rude to you. Your ego may even tempt you to throw your title around when life's eventual indignities strike. Honestly, I thought about it when I got towed for unwittingly leaving my car in a tow zone overnight. However, it doesn't pay to try to get anything out of public office other than the satisfaction of knowing you're making a difference. It's public service, not self-service, after all. Don't get too comfortable. There are just enough people who do follow local politics that you need to mind what you do and what you say in public.

Third, your entire life's rhythm gets thrown off when you become a local elected official. My life now revolves around the "battle rhythm" of the council schedule and our bi-monthly council meetings. Finish one council meeting and you're getting ready for the next one. You'll try your best to create stability in your life. Then, there'll be an officer-involved shooting,[52] the president will tweet about an undocumented immigrant who took a chainsaw to his significant other,[53] or perhaps a tree will fall on a wedding party.[54] As an elected official, you're just not entirely in control of your life anymore – there's no typical day – and it takes some time getting accustomed to that. Social media exacerbates matters, turning what once was a part-time volunteer gig into almost a full-time job. Theoretically, you could spend every waking hour on city matters. There is a never-ending amount of problems you could address or improvements you could pursue.

And that's just the official business of the council. You'll also quickly become swamped with requests to speak to various service and political clubs, and to attend fundraisers, dinners, and galas. You can't participate in everything. Don't even try. I accept invitations to attend events using two criteria. First, does this relate to an issue that's significant to me? Second, are the people inviting me going to appreciate my time? That means I'll attend most events looking to address the homelessness crisis and ignore invitations that reach me still addressed to the "Honorable Bob Henderson."

Make sure to take your mental and physical health seriously. This starts by sitting down with your loved ones and talking about how life might be changing. You'll need to get buy-in from your loved ones for your new endeavor and whatever strategy you choose to take for the early months of your tenure. If your habits have slipped during the election (it happens), make a plan for a better diet, exercise, and rest. Go back to church if you stopped. If you meditate, set aside time to recommit to your practice.

Be mindful of the impact of the campaign and of being an elected official on your family. In May of 2019, my incredible wife and ironwoman, Christina, was diagnosed with breast cancer.

Nothing can prepare you for something like that. You just never know what life will throw at you. Keeping your council role in perspective will go a long way toward warding off unnecessary stress. It'll also help you enjoy the limited time you have to enjoy with your loved ones on this earth.

What If You Lose?

Before I go any further, I should probably address the (other) elephant in the room. Remember how I said campaigning is an iterative process? That doesn't stop after the election, win or lose. The most important thing about losing an election is to take it as a learning lesson, albeit a painful one. It hurts to be rejected. It hurts exponentially more to be rejected by hundreds or even thousands of people. Try not to take it personal. Look at your loss as an opportunity to learn and improve.

If you do lose, don't rush right back into public life. Don't be the local face of the resistance. Don't sue the registrar (unless there was actual wrongdoing). Don't circulate a recall petition against the winning candidate. Take time to process the loss. Take a vacation. Go on a retreat. You might, after some time away, realize politics isn't right for you. There are plenty of ways to make a difference and give back, politics being just one. You might, after some quiet reflection, decide you want to give it another go. Take it slow. As the saying goes, "You've got to go away to come back." And when you do return, when you've learned a lesson and come back hungrier and better equipped to win, it'll be all the more enjoyable when you do. As poet Emily Dickinson wrote, "Success is counted sweetest / By those who ne'er succeed."

Stay in Office

In due course, you'll go from surviving the first days and months of your post-election life to surveying the horizon and wondering what else is possible. That can mean anything from full-time employment in government affairs to the state legislature or Congress. Some of you will be satisfied right where you are, hanging out in local government for the long haul. Others will have the itch to start empire building. Because the nature of politics is instability and competition, though, trying to get atop, and stay on top of, the heap is a time-consuming, complicated, and frustrating task. Proceed with due caution.

Perhaps the most challenging task for me was navigating the internecine conflict among the various political factions within my local party. My election to the city council represented a shock not just to Whittier's old guard but it was also a reversal of what the cadre of ambitious Democratic political activists in the area, several of whom later ran for state assembly at the first opportunity, expected.[55] This put me in the uncomfortable position of being a leader of a movement that wasn't fully ready to embrace me.

After the election, I was invited to a hotwash, or debrief, held at Sage and organized by various Democratic activists. They spent their time decrying what they characterized as fraud and underhanded tactics in the District 4 race. I posited that the next four years would be another tryout and that we had better focus on what local residents care about most, which, as I've explained, tend to be mundane, hyper-local matters. Through my comments, I attempted to frame the election in a way that would ensure the right lessons were learned and to invite the activists to fall in behind me. I was confident my vision had the best chance of long-term success. I received a cool response.

Whatever your local area's politics, you'll need to decide what factions you can afford to leave out of your governing coalition and which ones you need to keep in. There's a fashionable phrase today that goes, "Elections have consequences." That simply means some groups will inevitably be in a better position due to an election than others. Don't feel guilty about this. You can't make everyone happy. It's natural to conclude that those who didn't support you, and especially those who continue to oppose you, shouldn't get the benefit of your hard-earned win.

Still, don't be vindictive. Just because you didn't get support from a group or person during the campaign doesn't mean you should shut that group or person out. Otherwise, you'll find yourself on an island rather quickly. Remember, people deserve a second chance. And, more importantly, loyalty is born in unexpected places. There are no permanent enemies in politics. You might be surprised at the results when you allow former opponents to save face with you.

Even if you don't start empire building, be mindful of how future elections will impact you. You'll invariably be dragged into battles over endorsements, fundraisers, and other political and campaign functions. Some politicians love this activity. Others just want to help people and not play games. You must decide for yourself how deeply you want to get involved. For me, the answer was simple. I achieved success by appealing directly to the people. I chose to leave the drama to others and focus on governing.

This isn't to say you should be entirely agnostic toward the political vicissitudes. I do occasionally endorse candidates for office and attend various political fundraisers and events. When I do endorse someone, it's because I believe in what they stand for and because I feel they can win. I don't endorse people based solely on how it might benefit me politically. Regardless of how deep you get into the partisan weeds, try to look upon politics as you would any other craft. Get better at it through careful study and also get better connected. With all that said, sometimes you can't avoid a good fight. When that happens, make sure you play for all the marbles.

Stay Connected

Take the extra step of proactively engaging with your community once you've gotten a handle of your new role and feel comfortable speaking at public events. This can take many forms:, tabling at local events, organizing town halls, hosting Facebook talks, speaking with audience members before a council meeting starts, or sitting down for a meal with constituents. Make sure you're out there finding out what's happening in your community directly from voters. Stay active on Facebook and take the complaints you receive to heart. Take nothing personally and focus on helping your community. Without the ongoing support of your constituents, you're a sitting duck.

I don't advocate being available 24/7, though. If you're a working professional, you know too well the pitfalls of the always-on corporate culture in America. You'll want to set reasonable boundaries and expectations when it comes to getting in touch with you. While constituents have the right to expect access to you, that doesn't mean the access should be unlimited or unconditional.

Most people are pretty good about giving you space if you provide them with simple parameters. I list my cell phone number publicly because I want residents to be able to cut through the bureaucracy and call me right away if something urgent or important is going on. The reality, though, is that most local issues aren't that way. Most people email me. I usually forward their requests to our administrative secretary, who places the matters on my calendar in fifteen minute increments. I've also set up an autoreply with useful links so that constituents can handle routine issues on their own, like requesting traffic safety measures or filing a permit.

Since I have neither personal staff nor a budget of my own, what I end up doing with routine requests is delegate them to the City Manager. He assigns the tasks to subordinates or explains why whatever is being requested can't be done. Unlike being a councilmember, this is a full-time job. Don't hesitate to make staff earn their pay and bennies.

By the way, use your city email and calendar consistently so that you establish a record when people invariably question your decisions. Cities are frequently sued. Never put anything in writing you would be embarrassed to see in print. As a fellow Marine used to tell me, "If you think it's worth an email, make it a phone call or a face-to-face."

Stay Fundraising

In all likelihood, you'll have some campaign debt left over from the race. There's nothing wrong with hosting a fundraiser following your election to retire that debt. However, if you ran as a candidate who doesn't take money from special interests, don't turn around and start taking big checks from private interest groups. Instead, form a fundraising committee and get them to help you organize a grassroots fundraiser. We held an event marking the 100th day since my election. My committee sold tickets for $50 and we got over 150 people to attend. Ultimately, I decided to use the proceeds not to pay myself back but instead to use for communications with my constituents. Regardless, it's a good idea to provide people in the community who might not have followed your race or who supported another candidate a chance to get behind you. After all, you did something big by winning your race. It's worth taking the time to celebrate.

Stay Informed

If you enjoyed *A Millennial's Guide to Running for Office*, please signup to my email newsletter for the most up-to-date campaign best practices and additional resources. Just take a picture of the custom QR code below using your smartphone and fill in your name and email address. How millennial is that?

Conclusion

Above all, be patient with yourself. No one is a political god on day one. Like any job, it takes time to get a handle on what you're doing. Realize that you're going to make some mistakes and that there's going to be a significant learning curve. At the end of the day, the community is better off because you were elected. Treat the office with the respect it deserves, and in time you'll make a significant difference in the lives of many.

Taking the Oath

I think I'm gonna pass out.

These, again, are the words I think to myself as the crowd piles into council chambers. It's April 24, 2018, my first council meeting. I'm sitting in the front row with Christina. There's a buzz in the room. Some are angry about the so-called "bubble trouble." Others are there to congratulate Bob Henderson on his service to the city. When Bob speaks, he lectures me on how I should behave as a councilperson. I'm somewhat peeved, but then I think of my father and how proud he'd be, and I remember to smile. Bob's speech ends, mercifully, and it's my turn to get up and take the oath of office.

"I do solemnly swear to protect and defend the Constitution against all enemies, foreign and domestic," I begin. After Christina finishes swearing me in, I take my seat on the dais and wait for my turn to address the audience. When it comes, I take a long pause, perhaps uncomfortably long, drinking in the moment. The place is standing room only, filled with people invested in making our city better, representative democracy in action.

I think of a longtime activist and all-around good guy named Ted Snyder. He had planned to run for the District 2 seat before dying unexpectedly of brain cancer.[56] "You're next!" he shouted at me during a political event celebrating Josue's 2016 election just a couple of weeks before Ted passed away.

I look down and think about Ted and my dad. I wonder how

they would feel if they were here. I then smile, breaking my silence: "How cool is this?"

RESOURCES

For videos and photos from my swearing-in ceremony, instructions on how to purchase copies of *A Millennial's Guide* in bulk, and for an online companion course to this book, please visit authorhenrybouchot.com.

ACKNOWLEDGMENTS

First of all, a book like this is the culmination of years and years of personal and professional development, and the list of people to thank, including teachers, coaches, family members, colleagues, and friends, could potentially stretch to many pages. In the interest of brevity, I have done my best to limit myself to those who directly impacted the campaign, particularly in the months immediately preceding the election. I deeply apologize to anyone I may have left out. It is a critique of my memory, not your impact.

To start with, I would like to thank my opponents in the race: Bob Henderson, Irella Perez, Eric Leckey, and Vincent McLeod. To quote Lincoln, "We are not enemies, but friends. We must not be enemies."

My sincerest appreciation goes to those who shared the campaign trail with me as volunteers, as well as those who helped in the background. I have already mentioned Candi Nash, Gabriel Rodriguez, Daniel Malignaggi, and Caro Jauregui, but I also want to thank Erica Ortega, Kyle Davis, Lawrence Sanchez, Jose Luevano, Ricardo Pelaez, Jason Chacon, Niel Opdahl, Troy Chavez, Max Ordonez, Felicia Fierro, Henry Huerta and Sarah Matlock.

A special shoutout goes to those who organized fundraisers and meet-and-greets for me, including Eric Slatkin, Jim Scull, Don Deming, James Ramos, Mario Gras, Ted Gottis, Javier Quinones,

Theo Morga, Donna Hollander, John Young, Gary Couso-Vasquez, Guy Battaglia, Lorenzo Gomez, Rebecca Zapanta, and Pat Almada. I have a feeling I learned more from you than you did from me and I thank you for the opportunity.

Thank you to the local businesses in Whittier who helped me by allowing me to meet at their establishments, specifically: Local Fixture, the Deli Up, Greenleaf Thai Cuisine, the Knotted Apron, Spin Lounge, and Sage.

I owe a special debt of gratitude to those who provided me with advice and support leading up to the race. Our conversations helped more than you might realize: Anthony DiMartino, Christine Jerian, Ben Tarzynski, Camillo Cruz, David Levitus, Dotty Anderson, Eve LaDue, Greg Spiegel, Herlinda Chico, Angela Galanis-Price, Jose Del Rio, Megan Hobza, Lisa Dulyea, Malcolm Corona, Alex Vargas, Erin Tanenbaum, Paul Navarro, Ray Wong, Jeff Farber, Sandra Figueroa-Villa, Ted Knoll, Rachel Bailit, Alex Berrio Matamoros, Danielle Cendejas, Steven Otto, Lorraine Langevin, Jake Vollebregt, Jennifer Gordon, and John Beynon.

Many thanks to the editors and readers who helped me hone this book: Nathan Prorok, Emma Borges-Scott, Charity-Jean Conklin, Daniel Fierro, Nancy Olson, and Donald Weise.

Last but not least, thank you to every single person who made a contribution, large or small, and, most of all, to each of the 1,095 residents of Whittier who had enough trust in me to lead their city.

ENDNOTES

1 For more on this idea, check out Happy City: *Transforming Our Lives Through Urban Design* by Charles Montgomery.

2 https://www.whittierdailynews.com/2018/07/12/whittiers-3m-solution-for-local-homeless-should-extend-beyond-city-borders-council-members-say/

3 https://www.whittierdailynews.com/2019/03/20/skid-row-looking-homeless-encampment-pops-up-in-whittier-greenbelt/

4 https://www.whittierdailynews.com/2020/09/01/whittiers-new-homeless-shelter-opens/

5 https://www.pasadenastarnews.com/2020/09/27/whittier-finds-a-partial-homelessness-fix/

6 https://www.latimes.com/archives/la-xpm-1990-07-19-ga-555-story.html

7 https://www.latimes.com/archives/la-xpm-2008-mar-22-me-whittier22-story.html

8 https://www.whittierdailynews.com/2019/03/04/ex-whittier-couple-faces-trial-in-drowning-death-of-girl-whose-body-was-taken-to-mexico-in-bag/

9 https://www.whittierdailynews.com/2018/10/11/owner-of-richard-nixon-house-in-whittier-rebuffed-in-attempt-to-demolish-home/

10 https://www.latimes.com/local/bell/la-me-bell-scandal-a-times-investigation-20160211-storygallery.html

11 https://patch.com/california/baldwinpark/ex-el-monte-superintendent-awarded-700k-bullying-lawsuit

12 https://www.whittierdailynews.com/2020/03/04/whittier-election-surprise-republicans-now-have-4-of-5-council-seats/

13 See Odysseus in America by Jonathan Shay.

14 https://www.whittierdailynews.com/2015/11/15/kkk-propaganda-distributed-in-whittier-neighborhoods-for-second-time-this-year/

15 https://www.latimes.com/local/lanow/la-me-ln-kkk-propaganda-whittier-20150628-story.html

16 https://www.sgvtribune.com/2015/12/10/whittier-must-disavow-kkk-recruitment-attempt-letters/

17 https://www.whittierdailynews.com/2016/04/15/josue-alvarado-appears-to-have-won-whittier-city-council-election/

18 https://www.sacbee.com/news/politics-government/capitol-alert/article240816421.html

19 https://www.latimes.com/archives/la-xpm-2008-mar-22-me-whittier22-story.html

20 https://www.pasadenastarnews.com/2012/04/13/its-politics-whittier-city-council-election-shows-you-cant-underestimate-power-of-incumbency/

21 https://www.thecampaignworkshop.com/blog/political-campaign/political-consultant

22 https://www.whittierdailynews.com/2018/02/06/whittier-mayor-joe-vinatieri-leads-opponents-in-campaign-fund-raising/

23 https://www.whittierdailynews.com/2018/04/09/whittier-voters-must-sort-through-negative-campaigns-outside-money-in-tuesdays-city-council-election/

24 https://www.change.org/p/city-of-whittier-chairman-bob-henderson-stop-the-elimination-of-sunrise-to-sunset-hours-at-the-whittier-trails

25 https://www.nbclosangeles.com/news/gang-member-says-he-smoked-whittier-police-officer-cousin-in/18343/

26https://www.dailybreeze.com/2017/10/16/calling-it-another-three-strikes-law-gov-brown-vetoes-bill-proposed-in-wake-of-whittier-police-officers-death/

27 https://www.latimes.com/food/dailydish/la-dd-where-to-eat-whittier-20140226-story.html

28 https://www.sbsun.com/2011/08/25/update-whittier-activist-joe-marsico-dies-thursday-at-69/

29 https://www.whittierdailynews.com/2017/12/09/court-approves-settlement-allowing-development-of-nelles-prison-site-in-whittier-to-go-forward/

30 https://www.buzzfeednews.com/article/evanmcsan/scott-brown-trades-in-the-truck-in-new-hampshire

31 https://www.usatoday.com/story/news/politics/onpolitics/2016/05/04/ted-cruz-website-pro-hillary-endorsement/83949882/

32 https://www.whittierdailynews.com/2018/02/06/whittier-mayor-joe-vinatieri-leads-opponents-in-campaign-fund-raising/

33 http://www.thequakercampus.org/newsblog/tag/city+council

34 https://www.latimes.com/politics/la-pol-ca-tony-mendoza-harassment-resigns-20180222-story.html

35 https://www.latimes.com/archives/la-xpm-1992-04-23-hl-1633-story.html?fbclid=IwAR3Khefg9jKMHXOh-a7PXOkOv2OMbKnlF5wAofNBsSm56h4J-YEnBwlJ4Zc

36 https://www.projectmanagement.com/wikis/603813/7-38-55--Mehrabians-Rule-

37 https://www.dailynews.com/2006/01/24/candidate-makes-house-calls-to-win-more-votes/

38 http://fightcamp29.blogspot.com/

39 https://www.businessinsider.com/young-voters-dont-know-where-to-buy-stamps-for-absentee-ballots-2018-9

40 http://www.thequakercampus.org/newsblog/2018/2/15/an-interview-with-district-2-candidate-henry-bouchot

41 https://www.whittierdailynews.com/2018/04/25/the-whittier-election-isnt-over-attorney-demands-a-recount/

42 https://abc7.com/voting-ballots-whittier-election-confusing-ballot/3321261/

43 https://www.whittierdailynews.com/2018/05/09/facing-a-deficit-whittier-gets-by-one-more-year-without-spending-cuts-or-raising-taxes-heres-how/

44 https://www.whittierdailynews.com/2018/04/11/more-change-is-coming-to-whittier-city-council-after-tuesdays-election/

45 https://www.whittierdailynews.com/2020/04/29/they-said-what-at-the-whittier-city-council-meeting/

46 https://www.whittierdailynews.com/2019/03/11/whittiers-broadway-park-gets-a-refurbishment/
47 https://www.whittierdailynews.com/2018/11/24/the-man-who-nearly-single-handedly-saved-the-whittier-hills-may-be-leaving-the-board-that-oversees-them/

48 https://www.whittierdailynews.com/2020/09/01/whittiers-new-homeless-shelter-opens/

49 https://ktla.com/news/local-news/whittier-street-closed-to-allow-businesses-to-expand-outdoors-to-allow-for-social-distancing-at-greenleaf-promenade/

50 https://la.curbed.com/2020/2/27/21156253/metro-whittier-eastside-extension-train-gold-line

51 https://www.whittierdailynews.com/2019/09/28/photos-whittiers-first-ever-festival-celebrating-lgbtq-pride-held-at-central-park/

52 https://www.whittierdailynews.com/2020/04/30/whittier-police-involved-in-a-shooting-with-a-suspect/

53 https://abc7.com/chainsaw-attack-whittier-domestic-violence-alejandro-alvarez/3772896/

54 https://www.whittierdailynews.com/2017/04/05/family-of-woman-killed-in-penn-park-tree-collapse-on-wedding-party-sues-whittier/

55 https://www.whittierdailynews.com/2020/03/03/calderon-dynasty-at-stake-in-assembly-district-57-race/

56 https://www.whittierdailynews.com/2017/02/20/ted-snyder-whittier-conservancy-president-dies-at-65/

Made in United States
North Haven, CT
08 November 2024

60009245R00127